THE
GEORGIAN HOUSE
and its details

THE
GEORGIAN HOUSE
and its details

Richard Reid

Bishopsgate Press

To Tom and Monica

British Library Cataloguing in Publication Data

Reid, Richard,
  The Georgian house and its details
  1. Architecture, Domestic — Great Britain
  History 2. Architecture, Georgian — Great Britain
  I. Title
  728′.0941 NA7328

ISBN 0-900873-93-0

All enquiries and requests relevant to this title should be sent to the publisher, Bishopsgate Press Ltd., 37 Union Street, London SE1 1SE

Printed in Great Britain at The Bath Press, Avon

Contents

Author's Acknowledgements

This is a book by a practising architect who has noted down, from much reading and various travels, the architectural observations that seemed most pertinent to him about the design of the smaller houses and cottages of 18th century England.

I am not an architectural historian, and therefore my debt to many others whose scholarship over countless years makes such books as mine possible, is considerable. There is a complete bibliography at the end of this book, but I do owe a particular debt to the stimulating writings and lectures of Dr Ronald Brunskill; to Professor M.W. Barley's two books *The English Farmhouse and Cottage* and *The House and Home.* Professor Barley has allowed me to adapt a number of the drawings in his book for the purpose of this book of mine. I also acknowledge my debt to writings and/or illustrations in Robert Naismith's *Buildings of the Scottish Countryside;* Eric Mercer's *English Vernacular Houses* and Peter Smith's *Houses of the Welsh Countryside* and in books by Alec Clifton-Taylor, Gillian Darley, Dan Cruickshank, Estyn Evans, Colin Sinclair, Caoimhin O Danachair, A. Gailey, F.H.A. Aalen; and to the British Architectural Library, the Royal Commission on Historical Monuments and Her Majesty's Stationery Office.

I am most grateful to Ian Straker and Austen Smith of Bishopsgate Press for providing the opportunity for me to write such a book; to my colleagues in the practice for putting up with my book-cluttered studio. Especial thanks are due to Bridget Chilvers and Frankie Waterman who both typed the manuscript and helped in the picture research; and once again to my family who suffered the most, with the greatest of patience, whilst I worked on the book.

Introduction

Over the past twenty-five years or so, I have made countless drawings of vernacular building and architecture in various parts of the British Isles. Only in the last fifteen years have I begun to make a more rational analysis of the source and origin of this architecture inspired, primarily, by Dr R.W. Brunskill's marvellous book, *Illustrated Handbook of Vernacular Architecture,* first published by Faber and Faber in 1971.

My investigations became more urgent in recent years as the architectural practice to which I belong began to be more involved in housing design. I wanted to understand more about the traditional English house, and especially the relationship between vernacular building and architecture. By making the drawing of such buildings it was as if their requisite sense of scale and place might somehow be inculcated within one's own designs.

Looking through my sketch books, I found I had more than enough drawings, both descriptive and analytical, of the houses built in the 18th and early 19th centuries to make a more systematic study of a particular period in English Architectural History, when, for the first time, vernacular building found an appropriate architectural replacement in the invariably handsome smaller Georgian house and cottage. For me, such a beginning seemed a particularly pertinent place to start since today there is such pressure for architects to revert to a mere replication of such a past. Should such housing be modelled on a vernacular mould, or could it, in fact, be architecture?

In a particularly bitter attack, *British Architecture: Thirty Wasted Years* (Sunday Times, February 1977), Conrad Jameson wrote that the public today had little love for modern architecture. He argued that architects should now get out of public housing; that we should go back to pattern books for council housing, back to vernacular designs. He pointed out that the proliferation of traditional features on the designs of much new housing both in Britain and continental Europe provides ample evidence that the public has equally strongly-held views, and that if they cannot have the real vernacular, then they will quite happily settle for something that refers to it.

But why do people want these imitations? Herman Muthesius believed he had put his finger on this when he wrote in his book *The English House* (English translation by Crosby, Lockwood Staples, 1979) " ...the Englishman in his house wants peace. A tidy cosiness, fully developed comfort, that is what is important to him ...his unalterable preference is for the rural and rustic. Such accord seems to him to be a link with beloved mother nature, to whom, despite all high culture, the English nation has remained more faithful than any other people."

The widespread popularity of pseudo-vernacular today seems to be its dominant impression of unity, but, as Adrian Forty and Henry Moss pointed out (article in the Architectural Review, February 1980), this is only an illusion of harmony for "...pseudo-vernacular succeeds in incorporating a set of thoroughly discordant and disconnected social beliefs". The authors believe that it is exactly this provision that is the key to its success. The dominant image is one of villageness, an image which is at the heart of people's reasons for choosing such a place to live. The authors believe people see the village as "...the only setting in which authentic feelings and intimate and meaningful social relations are possible, and the picturesqueness of traditional villages is a metaphor for such virtues".

As Kenneth Clarke tells us in *Landscape into Art* (Penguin Books, 1956) the imagination of Renaissance artists was furnished by Virgil's myth of ideal rusticity. In creating this myth, Virgil, one of the great poets of antiquity, combined a first-hand knowledge of the country with the most enchanting dream which has ever consoled mankind, the myth of a golden age in which man lived on the fruits of the earth, peacefully, piously and with primitive simplicity - poetic as opposed to scientific truth.

The 17th century painter, Claude, was pre-occupied with the Virgilian myth - the elements of the Virgilian dream in Claude - Kenneth Clarke has pointed out, is his sense of a Golden Age, of grazing flocks, unruffled waters and a calm luminous sky, images of perfect harmony between man and nature, but touched, as he combines them, with a Mozartian wistfulness, as if he knew that this perfection would last no longer than the moment in which it takes possession of our minds.

18th century England is portrayed as such a Golden Age. When George I ascended the throne on September 18th 1714, Britain was overwhelmingly rural. As Michael Reed has observed in *The Georgian Triumph 1700-1830* (Paladin Books, 1984), there were 794 places in England and Wales deserving to be called towns, but of these only 400 had a population in excess of 700. Such towns were distinctive, living communities, as he writes, enhanced by the difficulties of travel. And the small size of such towns meant that "....the country was never far away. Fields and farms, the smell of new-mown hay, or of a farmyard midden, were the common experience of most townsmen. As late as 1800 there were cornfields within a quarter of a mile of Liverpool Town Hall".

One must remember that Virgil's work was written after the horrors of the Civil War. Gilbert Highet writes in *Poets in the Landscape* (Penguin Books, 1959) that one view of the period was that Augustus was a great man and Virgil, recognising that greatness, thought himself privileged to expound his ideals. A counter argument, he points out, however, was that Virgil was a miserable sycophant who accepted a bribe to become the propogandist of a velvet-gloved tyrant. The parallels with 1980's Britain seem all too obvious. As Adrian Forty and Henry Moss suggest "...through its power to create a scenery referring to ways of life that are believed to be harmonious and stable, architecture has often been used to give an appearance of order that conceals the conflicts at large within the enviroment". But in turning back to the past, contemporary architects were not searching for the source and origin of their architecture, in the functional and vernacular tradition epitomised by the Arts and Crafts movement in Britain, but were, instead, looking merely for a means of providing a *style* commensurate with the myth. The neo-vernacularists were intent on making a jelly mould of the vernacular, not learning from it.

The great Arts and Crafts architect, Edward S. Prior, wrote in an article *Church Building as it is and as it might be* (Architectural Review, Vol.IV, 1898) that Traditionalism was not the answer, "...the styles are dead ...such things are gone". He urged a return to the principles underlying the style, of going back to the simple necessities of Building and finding in them a power of beauty, a poetry without rhetoric. And as Lethaby remarked in his book *Architecture* (Williams and Norgate, London, 1911) "...the modern way of building must be flexible and vigorous, even smart and hard. We must give up designing the broken-down picturesque which is part of the ideal of make-believe".

The 18th century was the golden age of English house building of a quality of craftmanship and design the like of which had not been seen before. For the rising middle-class of the period, the handsome rectangular or square-fronted symmetrically planned houses were of the most modern and up-to-date design. They were, in a sense, architecture's answer to similar sized houses built in the vernacular tradition by previous generations. Small though many of the houses were, they still belonged to the Grand Design tradition. But whilst these two traditions were distinctly different, they were nevertheless related.

There is a pressure for architects today to draw closer to everyday reality, with a preference for popular and dialectical forms and the inevitable rejection of the abstract and exotic, as the Italian architectural historian, Leonardo Benevolo, has suggested (*The History of the Modern Movement,* Routledge and Kegan Paul, 1971). If this is so, then it doesn't seem unreasonable for an architect concerned with housing to begin such a re-examination of the source and origin of one's architecture in the heyday of English house building in the 18th century. After all, it was in the 18th century that many small houses, for the first time, could be conceived along either architectural or vernacular lines.

This book is a collection of essays based on the readings and travel sketches of a practising architect concerned with the relationship of building to architecture, a relationship made so poetic in 18th century England. Whilst fascinated by the larger Georgian houses, my particular concern here is with the smaller houses and cottages of the period, their construction and convenience, their furniture and fittings.

Eighteenth Century England

Abroad, Great Britain in the 18th century was largely preoccupied with the epic struggle with France for commercial and colonial supremacy in the New World and India. At home the 18th century was remarkable for the birth of the modern English landscape, a result of the extensive land enclosures by the Georgian planners, as well as for the transformation of England, due to the great Industrial Revolution, from an agrarian to a largely industrial nation.

A particularly idyllic picture of 18th century England is that portrayed by Thomas Gainsborough in his painting *Mr and Mrs Andrews* (1748–9). The couple are seated, on slightly rising ground, under the shade of a tree. In the foreground are corn fields; in the middle distance sheep graze in a field bounded by hawthorn; the horizon seems limitless. It is an enchanting work inspired by the 17th century Dutch landscape painters. Marvellous though the portrait of this particular couple is, it is the sensitively observed background that is also of great interest, for here is a painting of one of the *new* landscapes, complete with hawthorn hedge and painted during the great period of Georgian enclosures and subsequent merging of the farms. Mr and Mrs Andrews were clearly wealthy. This is a portrait, not simply of a landowning couple, but also of the land they owned, running, one imagines, to the horizon and beyond. Their farming methods are modern, as seen by their enclosures, and their capital is considerable, for such enclosures were costly. This picture is a portrait

Mr and Mrs Robert Andrews painted by Thomas Gainsborough (1717 - 1788) *(Mr G.W. Andrews collection).*

Picturesque poverty was idealized in both painting and literature.

of a wealthy and comparatively peaceful England. Gainsborough later wrote of his youthful period, that "... there was not a picturesque clump of trees, nor even a single tree of any beauty, no, nor hedgerow, stem or post in my native town that I did not treasure in my memory from my earliest days". This period was also the *golden age* of English house building with the design and craftsmanship in architecture and decorative art of an exceptionally high quality.

But there was, in stark contrast, another England also, peopled by small tenant farmers evicted from their lands or cottagers deprived of their grazing rights, due to the Georgian enclosures, swelling the growing army of rural poor. This was a time when the real poor had no political rights. In 1723 Parliament enabled parishes to collaborate in the establishment of a workhouse, with board for the inmates paid for by a local manufacturer in return for cheap labour. Children were ringed by the neck or manacled to prevent them absconding. In lean years, as J H Plumb has pointed out in *England in the 18th Century* (1963), "... the despair of the poor became unendurable; food riots, with burning, looting, and mob violence were commonplace. The militia suppressed them and hangings and transportations followed." Fear of the destitute was such that all parties believed that the savage laws dealing with crimes against property were justified so that, as J H Plumb has pointed out, "... by 1740, for stealing a handkerchief worth one shilling, so long as it was removed privily from the person, children could be hanged by the neck until dead."

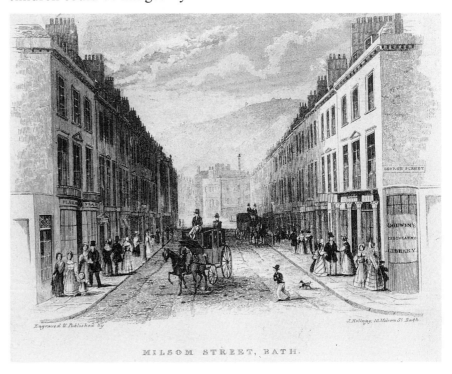

Milsom Street, Bath.

At the beginning of the 18th century, England, led by a Hanoverian monarch who hadn't taken the trouble to learn the language and who embroiled her in continental quarrels for which she had little taste, was a land of straggling villages and small hamlets; what towns there were were situated largely along the coast. Whilst towns of substance were beginning to grow in the north and midlands, the majority of the population, predominantly rural still, resided in the south. J H Plumb estimates the population in 1714 to be about five and a half millions. Whilst the population of East Anglia, whose prosperity during the late Middle Ages was based on the manufacturing revolution created by the Flemish Weavers, was on the decline, the population of the West Midlands, South Lancashire and the East Riding were on the increase. London, continuing the rapid expansion of the 17th century, had a population in excess of half a million; the population of flourishing commercial centres, such as Bristol and Norwich, had reached 50,000, whilst the sprawling industrial villages, such as Birmingham, Liverpool, Sheffield, Leeds and Halifax in the north, were growing

11

Houses in Salisbury Cathedral Close.

into sizeable towns. But such rapid expansion created its own problems – unpaved, narrow streets where most corners were made into a public convenience; dilapidated and overcrowded houses (in Manchester, ten persons to a room was typical), filth, squalor and disease. Many rooms were unfurnished, the occupants sleeping close together on a mattress of shavings. Diseases, such as smallpox, typhus, typhoid and dysentery, were commonplace. The infant mortality rate was so high that even in London only about one child in four survived.

The urban poor, marooned amongst death and despair, sought palliatives in drink and gambling, often errupting in inevitable violence. Constitutionally, most towns were mere villages, law and order being maintained by no more than two parish constables. Even in the larger corporate cities such as London and Bristol, the streets were unsafe, especially at night, with arson and looting, often by mobs, being commonplace. But despite the squalid conditions of most towns, there was an ever endless stream of emmigrants from the countryside flocking to the teaming streets and seedy tenements in search of work.

At the beginning of the 18th century, Gregory King estimated that over half of England and Wales was under cultivation as arable,

North Brink, Wisbech, Cambridgeshire.
Described by Pevsner as one of the most perfect
Georgian streets of England.

pasture or meadow, whilst some ten million acres was still "heaths, moors, mountains and barren lands". According to King, of the arable land, only half, some 4500000 acres, was enclosed in the kind of fields typical of today's landscape. The remainder was still largely medieval, with farming carried on in open fields that had changed little since the 13th century. The open field system had its deepest roots in the Midlands, as W G Hoskins has pointed out in *The Making of the English Landscape,* where most villagers lived and worked within the frame of a two-field or a three-field system. The enclosures of the Georgian planners had most effect in the large tract of central England. Essex and Kent were largely enclosed by the mid-16th century, but it was in counties such as Northamptonshire, Bedfordshire and Huntingdonshire to the east, Oxfordshire to the south and Rutland to the north, that the transformation from an ancient landscape to a modern one was most marked. It was here that the complex pattern of narrow strips and winding cart roads, surviving today in only a few places, such as at Laxton in Nottinghamshire and Brauton in Devon, gave way to a chequer-board pattern of small fields bounded by hawthorn hedgerows.

Georgian Architecture

Regularity and variety are the two inventive driving forces in 18th century English architecture. The century began, as Christopher Hussey has pointed out, witness to " . . . the most consistent attempt to conform English temperament to classical principles of thought and design". Examples are the bombastic brilliance of the great house by architects such as Vanburgh, Hawksmoor and Archer, the three major personalities of the short-lived English Baroque, or the harmonious proportions and refined detail of the Anglo-Palladian School, led by architects such as Lord Burlington, William Kent and Colin Campbell, with which it was superseded. By the close of the century, architects had begun to break away from such classical constraints in preference for picturesque irregularity as epitomized by Strawberry Hill, London, designed by Horace Walpole between 1747 and 1763, the first of the great Gothic Revival works.

Georgian architecture began comparatively modestly. The straightforward stone-dressed brick architecture of mid-17th century Dutch

Iver Grove, Buckinghamshire (1722).
Lovely five by three bay Baroque house with giant Doric pilasters supporting a three bay pediment.

Brick and stuccoed terraced houses, Chichester.

18th century terraces, Bradford-on-Avon.

Palladianism greatly influenced English domestic architecture after the Restoration in 1660. Such fresh influences were gradually assimilated until, by the turn of the century, a national character in English architecture was clearly formed.

The reign of Queen Anne (1702–14) was preoccupied abroad with the War of the Spanish Succession, in which England formed a Great Alliance with Holland, the Austrian Hapsburgs, Savoy, and Portugal, opposed to Louis XIV who, having accepted the throne of Spain for his grandson, Philip, was feared as a threat to the safety of other European nations. At home it was strife also, but between the revival political parties. The Whigs, composed chiefly of non-conformists, traders and the rising middle class, planned to curtail royal power in favour of Parliament; the Tories, consisting mainly of the landed gentry and clergy, advocated instead an extension of the Royal Prerogative. But it was for those same Whigs, whose wealth was based on the expanding trade with the New World and the East during the ensuing peace, that the majority of Early Georgian country houses were built.

The Queen Anne House (1702–1714)

Unlike the larger country houses of the period with their boldly articulated facades and principle floors generally raised above a semi-basement or ground storey, the smaller town houses, known as Queen Anne, were comparatively conservative in character. Preserving much of the form and detail of their late 17th century predecessors, these houses have an easy-going classicism, greatly admired by the Edwardians on which they modelled their country houses. The well built brick facades are generally symmetrical, consisting of two principle storeys, with equal sized windows on both floors. Sometimes the ground floor is raised above a semi-basement, whilst a projecting string course articulates the floors. Generally there is a steeply pitched, hipped roof containing an attic storey, lit by dormer windows. The tiled roof has a projecting eaves cornice, whilst the chimney would be articulated with panelling. Because of the fire risk in London the use of a wooden eaves cornice was made illegal, to be replaced by a simple brick parapet. Decorative quoins or angles were highlighted by the use of stone or different coloured brick. Many entry porches were quite ornate consisting of projecting canopies carried on highly decorative corbels. The entrance door was invariably flanked by pilasters, whilst the canopies above were either straight, sometimes with a fanlight above the door to light the hallway, or hooded, the latter often being formed with a decorative shell-like soffit. The smaller houses generally

Fenton House, Hampstead.
Built in 1693, this fine Queen Anne house has the homely classicism much admired by Edwardian architects.

Mompesson House, Salisbury.
Built in 1701, it is part of a group of fine Georgian houses built in Salisbury Cathedral Close.

made do with a simpler wood door frame of engaged columns and pedimented entablature. There was often a short flight of three or four steps to the entrance door.

Good examples are Fenton House, Hampstead (1693), Mompesson House, Salisbury (1701) and No 42 Queen Anne's Gate, London (1693). The larger of these houses, such as the seven bayed Fenton House, sometimes had a slightly projecting central section crowned by a graceful pediment. The Swan House, Chichester (1711), is an equally handsome rectangular block of gauged and rubbed brickword with a moulded brick cornice crowned by a panelled parapet. The central bay, composed of three narrow lights above the segmentally pedimented entrance, projects slightly forward. Other examples include, the Moot House, Downton, Wiltshire (1650, re-modelled 1720), a five bay brick facade in Flemish bond, with a projecting central bay articulated by stone dressings and crowned by a pediment and Eagle House, Mitcham, Surrey (c 1700).

The major innovation was the introduction of sash windows. The earliest sash windows were rather clumsy affairs, constructed of large wood sections. Originally introduced from Holland in the late 17th

The Moot House, Downton, Wiltshire (1650, remodelled 1720).
Handsome, moderate-sized, five bay house, with centrally projecting single bay entrance crowned by a pediment.

century, they consisted of two panels, the top one fixed, the lower sash movable. But the earlier windows had no weights. Notches were made in the grooves to keep the sash window at a particular height by pegs. The sash windows were often inserted in the front facade only, whilst hinged iron casements were inserted in the rear, side and dormer windows.

Internally the panelling of rooms was less heavy handed than the interiors of the Stuart period. The preference, typical of the early Georgian period, was for plain borders and slightly recessed panelling. By the mid-18th century, the preference was for decorative wallpaper. Pilastered chimney pieces with cornices carried on consoles were characteristic, whilst ceilings were generally plain, often bordered by a cornice.

The Early Georgian House (1714–60)

As Defoe pointed out, trade was the primary source of England's wealth in the early 18th century. But at the beginning it was not easy, with many restrictive measures on the export of manufactured goods, inadequate capital and poor technology, as well as the deplorable state of transport. The restrictive measures were removed by Walpole in order to encourage trade, but the cost and difficulty of transporting goods was high. Most roads followed the prehistoric ridge ways or the ancient Roman roads or ran alongside the thousands of miles of the *boundaries* of the new estates colonized by the enclosures. Roads were virtually impassable for many months of the year, their upkeep dependent entirely on the inhabitants of local parishes. Inland, the principle method for transporting goods was by packhorse, which was extremely expensive. Worse, such roads were the haunt of highwaymen, the bain of travelling merchants.

The waterborne trade along the rivers and coasts flourished, however, with revenue being spent deepening the rivers and cutting canals which, with locks and sluices, brought trade eventually to many inland towns. Road transport improved to once inaccessible regions, with the passing by Parliament of numerous private acts called Turnpike Trusts. These Trusts were formed by entrepreneurs who charged a fee for the maintenance of whole sections of road.

The Whigs, having won the general election in 1715, the beginning of a 47 year rule of England, were anxious to extend the political and commercial power of England at almost any price, including war. The rapid commercial expansion under their government was extremely rich and varied. Long before the inventions of such as Arkwright's water frame 1769, Hargreaves' spinning jenny 1770 and Compton's mule 1779, there had been an active search for technological improvements in the form of a spinning machine from which the textile industry would flourish.

The demand for coal in the early 18th century was so enormous that available supplies were quickly exhausted, despite the fact that some landlords were happy to uproot home and garden in search of accessible seams. But the invention of the steam pump by Savery and Newcomen enabled mines to be dug deeper without fear of flooding, thus securing the foundation of one of England's most important basic industries. The expansion of the iron industry was another major development. The rapidly dwindling forest land, denuded by the iron industry in search of charcoal for smelting the iron, had severely damaged the industry in the early 18th century. But its fortunes were quickly revived by the enterprising Darby's of Coalbrookdale who were using coke to smelt iron by 1713. It was the new merchant princes and rising middle class, mostly Whigs, who benefited most from such

Shanngrove, Co. Limerick. Built in 1709, it shows that Dutch influence was still strong in provincial Ireland in the early 18th century. Flanking wings were added in 1723. The main difference between this building and many of the larger vernacular buildings is the verticality of proportion here and the ornamental chimneys.

19

Swanton Farmhouse, built 1719 at Bredgar, Kent. Marvellously virtuoso design in polychrome brick of five bays with ingeniously upward curving parapet accommodating a third storey in the central section. The giant pilaster strips at the side are, as Kerry Downes has pointed out in *English Baroque Architecture,* the most frequently vernacularized Baroque device, "...in some cases quotation replaced imitation".

industriousness, both intent on endowing themselves with the necessary social prestige, the former investing in large estates and fine country houses, the latter in elegant town houses. This was the period of the Grand Tour, for the well to do as well as aristocrat. Such travels not only pin pointed new markets for English goods, it enabled the more enterprising to learn from European agricultural, manufacturing and craft practice, at the time considerably in advance of English efforts, as well as to study European art and architecture. The fruits of such study, especially the latter, were quickly evident as the returning traveller, equipped with the visual vocabulary of the classical civilization, began to seek his own equivalent in his own surroundings.

In the early 18th century, hygiene was of a deplorable standard with water drawn from rivers and houses drained into the streets. Home remedies and magic charms, offered as cure-alls for problems from rheumatism to venereal disease, impeded the development of medical science. The poor, incarcerated in the filth and disease-ridden urban slums, starved whilst the upper classes grew gross on vast quantities of food. Much-needed social change was slow, the new wealth being spent on more visible symbols of success, the elaborate mansions springing up in lush park-like settings, their architecture influenced by experiences of the prescribed Grand Tour of Europe.

**Pickhill Hall, Sesswick, Denbighshire.
The Italian influence, for many larger houses in the early 18th century, was for a flat front, the roof hidden behind a parapet or balustrade, as in this example.**

20

The Lions, Bridgwater, Somerset.
Built c.1730 by Benjamin Holloway, a carpenter and builder, it is an ambitious two storey house raised above a basement storey and flanked by projecting single storey pavilions.

The architecture of the short-lived English Baroque (1695–1725), was comparatively restrained in comparison with its European contemporaries. Examples include Castle Howard, Yorkshire (1699–1712), Blenheim Palace, Oxfordshire (1702–20) and Seaton Delaval, Northumberland (1720–28), all by Sir John Vanburgh, the former soldier and playwright. But to contemporaneous English taste, these houses were remarkably monumental, as well as vividly dramatic in conception. Such architectural extravagance was soon supplanted, however, by the calmer classicism of the Anglo-Palladian phase precipitated by increased interest in architecture of the wealthy social groups surrounding such figures as the Earl of Burlington, the Anglo-Palladian school's most influential advocate.

Ivy House, Chippenham, Wiltshire. Built c.1730, it is a fine Baroque house, with recessed centre and short, projecting wings, each crowned with a large segmental pediment.

The sudden interest in architecture during this period was inspired, not only by increased travel, but by the publication of numerous scholary books on architectural design. The most influential books were *Vitruvius Britannicus,* published in 1717 and 1725 by Colin Campbell, the architect of Mereworth House and many others, a new edition of Palladio's *I quattro libri dell 'Architettura,* published under the title *The Architecture of A Palladio* by Giacomo Leone between 1715 and 1716, and the description of Palladian design principles in *Rules for Drawing Several Parts of Architecture,* published by the Scots architect, James Gibbs in 1732. This latter was an influential pattern book used not only by architects but also by master builders and craftsmen, not only here, in England, but in America as well.

21

Bellmont Forest, Co. Cavan. Designed c.1730 by Sir Edward Lovett Pearce, it is one of the earliest Palladian houses in Ireland. Remarkably austere villa block with facades divided into bold articulated horizontals.

Mount Kennedy, Co. Wicklow. Designed by James Wyatt in 1722. Perhaps because one has become so accustomed to the aura of starkness and austerity within Ireland's vernacular tradition such amazingly restrained Neoclassical buildings such as this seem far more at home here than in England.

The Anglo-Palladian architecture is seen at its best in such houses as Chiswick House, London (1725) and Holkham Hall, Norfolk (1734), both by William Kent in collaboration with Lord Burlington, Mereworth Castle, Kent (1722-25) by Colin Campbell and Prior Park, Bath (1735–48) by John Wood the elder. All are re-interpretations of the great houses of the 16th century Italian architect, Andrea Palladio. In fact, Mereworth Castle and Chiswick House are closely modelled on Palladio's Villa Capra Vicenza, each with their elegant piano nobile level and domed central hall. But such houses were more suited to the Veneto region of northern Italy, where the climate was more congenial than that of England. These houses generally have solid, rather austere exteriors contrasting starkly with richly decorated interiors. The medium-sized Palladian house generally consists of a simple rectangular block, minus wings. The principal rooms, planned around a spacious central hall, are raised above a basement storey containing kitchens and ancillary accommodation. Bedrooms were on the first floor, whilst attic space was for additional servants' quarters. There were no bathrooms, a large tin bath sufficing, with hot water ferried to it in cans carried by the servants. The closet, generally a wood seat over a cess pit, was invariably positioned in the back yard or garden.

22

Palladian architectural principles were applied not only to the grander country mansions and houses of the period, but also to the relationship of one building to another within the towns and cities of the period. Good examples are the works of John Wood the elder (1704–54) and John Wood the younger (1728–81) in Bath. Here they developed an architectural strategy linking numerous town houses in grand crescents and squares. Whilst the facades of such terraces, often complete with pedimented central sections and flanking wings with shallow projections, recall palatial palace facades, the urban forms of the blocks are very much those of Ancient Rome. Notable examples of such 18th century civic design in Bath are The Circus, begun in 1754 by John Wood the elder and the Royal Crescent, built between 1767 and 1775 by John Wood the younger.

Crescent, Bath by W. Watts.

Early 18th century house, Weldrake, Yorkshire.
Four bay, brick house, with one gable end and
one hipped end to the pantiled roof. A projecting
brick cornice divides the two floors.

The gradual spread of wealth, however, affected the design and
detail of the smaller house too. Whilst the much needed improvement
in the standard of housing for the farm labourers and industrial
workers was slow, the rising middle class were soon comfortably
housed in small, but handsome Georgian houses built within the
expanding towns or in the countryside nearby. Similar in plan, they
were decoratively less ornate and also much smaller than the medium-
sized Palladian house. Square or rectangular in plan, they invariably
had a central entrance hall. Most were two storeys in height,
occasionally with an attic storey, in continuation of the Queen Anne
tradition. Characteristic was a projecting parapet, to hide the roof,
articulated by a projecting cornice. Chimneys were usually built
within the thickness of the flanking walls, the chimney breast thus
projecting into the rooms. The resulting recess on either side was
invariably appropriated for shelving or cupboard space. The
speculative-built terraced houses of the period were characterised by
narrow frontage, deep plans, many terraces being of two or three
storeys, generally raised above a basement level.

The Mid-Georgian House (1750–80)

Whilst many houses based on Palladian precedent were still being built, the younger, more progressive architects began to search further afield, as well as back in time, for inspiration, first to the Gothic, then to Rome and Greece to study architectural antecedents. Whilst the Palladian movement was based originally on an architecture inspired by Roman models, the younger architects now began to study more closely the original source and origins.

Numerous books were published, both here and abroad, of such archaeological investigations. Some of the most stimulating for English architects were Robert Wood's *Ruins of Palmyra,* published in 1753 and his *Ruins of Balbec,* published in 1757, or a series of volumes on Greece, published over the years by Nicholas Revert and James Stuart, beginning with *The Antiquities of Athens,* published in 1762, and probably their most influential volume.

The most influential architecture of the mid-18th century was an amalgam of ancient Roman and Palladian models. Leading exponents were such architects as Sir Robert Taylor, the most influential figure in London and the surrounding countryside, James Paine who, in a dozen mansions in the midlands and north, was softening the austerity

Ynysmaengwyn, Tywyn, Merioneth.
Handsome mansion, with pedimented central section, built 1758.

25

of Palladian facades by Rococo articulation, and Sir William Chambers (1723–96), the most inspired of the three who, in 1759 published *A Treatise on Civil Architecture.* His house designs were more refined than either Taylor's or Paine's and also more strictly Roman in origin. He was also the leading authority on chinoiserie, having published the results of three trips to China in a volume titled *Design for Chinese Buildings,* in 1757. A contemporary was the famous Robert Adam (1728–92), whose researches and designs were to radically change the face of late Georgian architecture. The great dialectical debate of the period, both in Britain and abroad, was whether the source of Classical design should be Roman or Greek. For Robert Adam the controversy was irrelevant, for he saw the possibility of a synthesis between both.

House plans were changing. The Great Hall was supplanted by a smaller hall with encircling reception rooms. Principal rooms were on the ground and first floors. Kitchens were generally situated in such a position that smells of cooking did not pervade the principal room, but their planning was inconvenient, the food having to be carried along numerous cold passages, making it difficult to keep the food hot. Servants ate in the kitchens; their bedrooms were in the attics.

The typical country cottage, gradually being built of more permanent materials in the affluent parts of England, still consisted of one main room. Some examples have parlours as well. Farmhouses had large kitchens to live and sleep in with adjoining scullery and

Plasgwyn, Pentraeth, Anglesey.
Mid 18th century red brick mansion with pedimented central section.

26

Cleeve Prior, Top Farm, Worcestershire. Small, three storey brick farmhouse with stone quoins, built in the mid 18th century.

larder. The larger farmhouses would generally have a separate parlour, whilst bedrooms in the roof were connected one to the other. The square, more symmetrical plans of the smaller country houses generally had a dining room and drawing room, as well as kitchen, pantry and butlery on the ground floor. Access to the bedrooms, unlike the long, one room wide plans of the neighbouring farmhouses, was from a spacious landing off the centrally-positioned stair.

The smaller Georgian houses gradually lost the traditional Queen Anne appearance with the disappearance of the classical pilasters and entablatures. Facades were much plainer, enlivened mainly by string courses and well-positioned window and door openings. Characteristic of many country towns are houses built of a mellow coloured brick, the angles and window surroundings picked out in a more vivid red brick. Window openings were generally varied to accentuate the importance of particular floor levels, so that the principal floor of the larger houses has taller, more elegant windows than the ground floor, and so on. Most of the smaller, predominantly two-storey houses of the villages and towns of the countryside have equally proportioned windows for both floors, usually consisting of six panels per sash. The glazing bars are now much thinner than those of the late 17th century. Most of the surrounding window frame is revealed. The simplicity of the fenestration is enhanced by the decorative elegance of the entrances. Typical is a panelled entrance door flanked by pilasters of

27

engaged columns supporting either a curved or triangular pediment. Fanlights above the door are normally semi-circular.

It was the Romans who first made window glass in this country. Window glass was re-introduced during the early Middle Ages. The glass of the 16th and 17th centuries was produced by the cylinder method, in which molten glass was blown first into a sphere and then, by the glass maker swinging and twisting the pipe, finally into a sausage shape which was then cut, left to cool and flattened. In the 18th century the more expensive crown glass was introduced for windows. Used for windows up to the early 19th century, crown glass was blown in circular sheets, some 5 feet in diameter. The panes cut from these sheets are characterized by a ripply surface, the concentric rings of the circular sheet, and has a pale, bluish tinge, a result of impurities in the silica sand. Some buildings of the period still have their crown glass.

Up to the mid-18th century the principal rooms were generally panelled throughout but this practice was gradually replaced by the use of sunken panels of plain boards below a dado rail. Later practice omitted all but the dado rail, which was retained to protect the walls from being scraped by the backs of chairs. In the larger houses, the height of fashion was the stretching of textiles on a frame fixed above the dado rail. In smaller, less affluent households, the hanging of wallpapers was more typical, particularly in the bedrooms. Another practice of the time was that of colour washing the walls, where there was no decorative panelling. Blue was a particularly favourite colour as it enhanced the dark mahogany furniture of the period.

Ickworth House, Suffolk, 1792. Impressive domed rotunda standing at the centre of a semi elliptical single storey corridor linking flanking two storey wings. Designed by Francis Sandys for Frederick Hervey, 4th Earl of Bristol and Bishop of Derry, a man with a vast income able to indulge his interest in architecture.

The Later Georgian House (1770–1800)

The creative genius of late 18th century English architecture was Robert Adam. The brother of John and James, they had continued the large Scottish practice of their father, William Adam, for nearly a decade before Robert, fresh from the Grand Tour, arrived in London in 1758. His work is a marvellous fusion of Greek and Roman architecture, combined with a considerable knowledge and understanding of the Renaissance. Great delicacy was added by decorative features re-interpreted from Greek vases and Roman frescoes often rendered in a striking combination of red, yellow and black, as in the decorative scheme for Osterly Park. He referred to such decorative detail as Etruscan. And it was this same Etruscan theme that Josiah Wedgwood (1730-95), one of the early industrial capitalists of the period, adopted for his pottery. He went so far as to name his factory, founded in 1769, Etruria.

The East side of St Andrews Square, Edinburgh, by Thomas E. Shepherd.

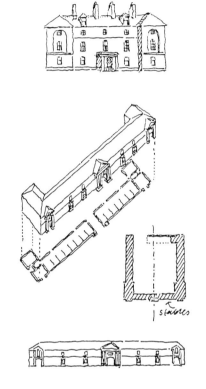

The influence of the discreet Adam Style, was greatly enhanced by the publication of the first two volumes of *Works in Architecture of Robert and James Adam,* (1773 and 1779), There refined and graceful architecture employed the symmetry and proportioning of contemporaneous work, but treated ornament in a freer, more daring manner. This was in complete contrast to the correct, but rather dour classicism of Sir William Chambers, Robert Adam arguing that the Romans, in preference to the temple architecture used externally for their houses, chose a more colourful, decorative interior. Whilst the work of Robert and James Adam was provided primarily for the rich, its influence was widespread, their characteristic details being copiously copied by the builders of smaller houses and terraces. Robert Adam standardised a range of decorative details and ornamental design most vividly for entrances, fireplaces, ceilings and wall friezes. The ingenuity of these compositions was such that moulds could be formed and the details applied permanently, resulting in the mass production of stick-on-mouldings by many manufacturers. Characteristic are entrances articulated by engaged columns, with any glazed opening above or flanking the door utilizing cast lead glazing bars. The Venetian window, composed of three lights, is a rich addition, whilst many ground storeys have a stucco surface, scored and painted to look like stone in the manner of the rusticated basement storeys of Renaissance palazzi.

Most memorable are the Adam interiors, with their unusual shaped circular, oval or apsidal ended rectangular rooms. Decorative work

West facade of Whim, near Leadburn, Peebleshire (a) a country house designed by William Adam in 1733 for the Earl of Kay, later the 3rd Duke of Argyll. In 1729, the Earl had embarked on a remarkable agricultural experiment which included the laying out of a model farm. The central three bays formed the original core of the house. The projecting end bays were added in the late 18th century. The court of offices, including stables, known as Whim Square (b) were laid out in the late 18th century. The entrance facade, on the west side, contains the stables designed to screen the court beyond. The ranges to the north and south contain farm buildings and cottages.

George Street, St Andrews Church and Melvilles Monument, Edinburgh, by Thomas H. Shepherd.

Lowther Village, Cumbria. Designed by the Adam brothers for Sir James Lowther from the 1760s onwards.

exploited low relief: ceilings were painted in pastel colours whilst largely white stucco decoration was highlighted by touches of gilt. Typical motifs are groups of flutes, pendants, wheat-ear and the anthemion, or Greek honeysuckle. Characteristic of chimney friezes and architraves to doors is a plaque decorated in low relief, either with a classical figure or festoon of wheat-ear. The principal rooms generally had a low dado rail, painted, whilst the walls themselves were generally colourwashed. Additional enrichment includes the use of arches and curved niches.

There was a considerable expansion in domestic building during this period. Whilst the scale of aristocratic mansions grew less grand, domestic buildings proliferated, as did the houses built to accommodate the rising middle class. Numerous villas were being erected on the outskirts of many towns by the late 18th century in either a classical or picturesque Gothic style, whilst even the humble cottages of the farm labour or the terraces of the industrial worker were being built of more permanent materials.

30

18th century cottages built alongside the village green, Groombridge, Kent.

Beaufort Square, Bath, designed by John Strahan between 1727-36.

18th century square, Bridgewater.

18th century terraces in the High Street, Modbury, Devon.

Industry

Whilst industrial life was beginning to change long before the mid-18th century, so violent and rapid was the pace of change between 1760 and 1790 that one now had two worlds, the old and the new, the old imbued with certain patrician values, the new stamped irrevocably as a product of technological change. Although the age of Walpole (1714–42) witnessed a rapid expansion of British trade with the opening up of lucrative markets both at home and abroad, the greatest change occured with the Agrarian and Industrial Revolutions begun in the age of Chatham (1742–84) and reaching its peak in the age of Pitt (1784–1815). The result was a huge shift in population from the south and east to the north and west, that most profoundly changed the face of working class and lower middle class Britain.

In the late 17th and early 18th centuries, the character of industrial workers' housing was little different to the habitat of crofters and cottagers. The scale of manufacture, until the mid-18th century, was comparatively small. For the worker in the tin mines of Cornwall or the lead mines of Derbyshire, mining and farming formed a twofold economy. It was the same in the uplands of West Yorkshire where farming was combined with weaving. Whilst the cloth trade began to expand in the late 17th century, many clothiers, not wishing to disrupt family life too much, often converted their existing kitchens into a

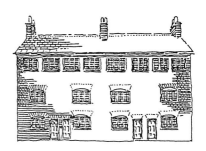

Terrace of four, three storey stocking-frame knitters' cottages, Stapleford, Nottinghamshire. Characteristic are the multiple lights of the top storey, front and back. Other interesting industrial buildings here of the late 18th century and early 19th century. The counties of Leicestershire and Nottinghamshire were the principle hosiery centres of the 18th century. These purpose designed terraces allowed stocking knitters to work from home, their stocking-frames accommodated in the well-lit top floor.

Port Ramsay, Lismore, Argyll, consists of a single row of limestone quarry workers' dwellings standing near the water's edge. Built in the early 19th century.

**Ashley Cottages, Carlops, Peebleshire.
Single storey weavers' cottages built in the late
18th century. The roofs were originally pantiled.**

workshop and then built a new kitchen in an extension to the rear of their dometic quarters. Such early adaptations were generally in rural areas. But as the factory system, one of the marked characteristics of the Industrial Revolution, gradually began to replace individual craft work, so the character and form of industrial workers' housing began to change.

The decline of the death rate due, (amongst other things,) to improved midwifery, resulted in a marked population growth which acted like a tonic on the British economy. The new industrialists, most emerging from the rapidly expanding lower middle classes, such as Arkwright, Peel, Watt, Wedgwood and a score of others, as J H Plumb points out, were not slow to exploit such a golden opportunity, aided and abetted by adequate capital and expanding markets.

Arkwright's water frame (1769), Hargreave's spinning jenny, invented in 1764 and patented in 1770, and Crompton's spinning mule (1779) revolutionized the production of yarn and brought to the weaver "an age of golden prosperity which was to last for a quarter of a century". But it was the loom and not the cotton mill that attracted immigrants in their thousands. The old loom shops could not cope, so new weavers's cottages with loom shops were built. These cottages, usually built of millstone grit, had a long range of windows on the upper floor to let in the maximum light. The space was unobstructed; there was good provision for storage and access for goods and

32

workers. In some existing houses the roof was converted into a weaving loft or a two storey workshop might be added. For many, small-scale farming, vegetable gardening, harvest work, etc, provided supplementary earnings.

During the first decade of the 19th century, census returns show that the population of England and Wales had increased from 9,168,000 to 10,488,000. While London, the largest city in Europe at the time, had a population of over a million people, the major growth was in the north and west. But while Manchester, with a population of 137,207 and Sheffield, Halifax, Leeds and Birmingham were expanding rapidly, the largest proportion of the industrial population was scattered throughout the northern countryside, housed in villages grouped around the mills sited alongside the streams and rivers of the Pennines, the source of their power. It was the invention of the power-loom, driven by water, which made all this possible. But whilst great fortunes were to be made by industrialists prepared to embrace the new methods, small enclaves of old-fashioned industrial ways of working lingered on side by side with the new technological ones.

For decades, as J. H. Plumb has pointed out, the industrial revolution was predominantly rural. The social consequences were often less than pleasant resulting in a new feudalism in which the mine or mill replaced that of the castle as the centre. The dependence of the workers on the mine or mill owner for their houses, shops, even

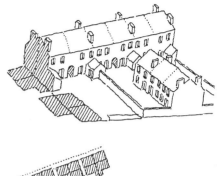
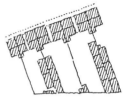

The archetypel back-to-backs. This example of early industrial housing was built in Birmingham in the early 19th century. Housing was built in a variety of patterns in the often awkward triangles of space left over behind the street frontages. Access to them was via passages through the main street frontages. When the countrymen flocked to the industrial towns in search of work from the late 18th century, housing such as this was built to accommodate them. Back-to-backs were virtually unknown in the South of England. They were built in the industrial cities and towns of the Midlands and North between the late 18th and mid 19th century.

Weavers' cottages at Jackson Bridge, West Yorkshire.
Built c.1800, the terraces are a small-scale development typical of the industrial expansion in the region.

Weaver's house built at Longley, Huddersfield, West Yorkshire, c.1800.
The weaver's loft is characterised by the multiple lights under the eaves.

chapels and schools, led, in many instances, to their exploitation, the recalcitrants being comparatively easy to discipline. The ending of the French wars created mass unemployment, forcing many to flee to the blast furnaces, cotton mills, coal mines and boom towns of the industrial north. While the non-industrialised communities of East Anglia and south east England continued to build the traditional cottages, the urban industrial worker was crammed into terraced cottages or the notorious rows of back-to-back housing of the early 19th century.

Communications

Apart from the Romans', as W. G. Hoskins has pointed out in *English Landscapes,* no national system of main roads was ever thought out in this country. Prior to the Conquest, the principle network consisted of broad, prehistoric trackways, such as the famous Jurassic Way, dating back to the Iron Age, combined with smaller more localised paths or tracks winding their way between one village and the next. The latter, typical of the Anglo-Saxon world, was extended following the Conquest as many existing towns grew in local or national importance whilst many new towns were planned. The pattern of inter-village paths was gradually extended into a network of primary routes at the centre of which was London. Whilst many roads, such as the Great North Road running out to the Scottish borders, spring from this period, their line was rarely finalised, for numerous were the diversions and re-routing to accommodate – first, a complex of monastic buildings and, second, re-alignments necessary to placate the aesthetic predelictions of the owner of some great country house intent on tidying up or extending his landscaped grounds.

There was also the network of wide grassy tracks called *drove roads,* along which the cattle and sheep were driven first from one pasture to another for fattening and then, later, to the markets of the Midlands and London. Most notable are the routes crossing the Cheviots from Scotland to England: the so-called Banbury Lane, connecting the pastures of the Welland Valley in the north-east midlands with the markets of Banbury in the south-east and the Welsh Road, sweeping across the Welsh Border into the flatter lands of Buckinghamshire.

When Celia Fiennes travelled the country on horseback in the late 17th century she described some roads as being " . . . so narrow and deep that an army could march unobserved, and so narrow that even single horses could scarcely pass each other."

The new commercial interests of the mid 18th century demanded speedy travel which the existing network of badly maintained roads and tracks was ill-equipped to deal with. Whilst much was transported by rivers or canals, many regions were still comparatively inaccessible. The new industrialists brought all their influence to bear on the Turnpike Trusts in order to radically improve the standard of road engineering. For much of the year the existing roads were a wilderness of bog and swamp, with merchants prey to highwaymen. Via a series of private acts, the more enterprising were able to take charge of the maintenance of whole sections of road, for which they duly charged a fee. Old roads were improved and straightened in sections, but such

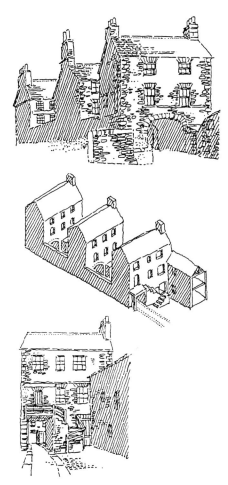

Kendal, the largest town in Westmorland, was a weaving centre from the 14th century, and prospered considerably in the 17th and 18th century. New Bank Yard, illustrated, was typical of the narrow lanes and yards with stone built workshops above, running at right angles from the main street, down to the River Kent.

Main Street, Campbeltown has some interesting late 18th century town houses. Nos. 50-52 are a three storey block, L-shaped in plan to the rear with a turnpike stair in the inside angle. (a); Nos. 58-72 were built in 1813 (b); Both groups of houses are stucco fronted.

Lock - keeper's house, Twelth Lock, Grand Canal, Co. Dublin. Built in the mid 18th century with huge blind arches articulating the facades, the front facade with giant keystone and gabled roof with encirculating cornice forming an austere pediment.

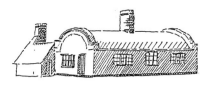

Barrel-vaulted lock-keeper's cottage built c.1815, alongside the Stratford-on-Avon Canal at Lowsonford, Warwickshire. One of many along this stretch of canal, built by the navvies for their own occupation.

improvements were slow.

In 1754 the journey by road from London to Manchester took four and a half days; by 1788 such were the improvements in road engineering that the journey time was reduced to two and a half days. Great improvements were made following the introduction of the Mail Coach in 1784 and the improvement in stage coach services in response to such competition. River traffic was important in Roman and medieval England and by the beginning of the 17th century there were about seven hundred miles of navigable rivers, mostly in Southern England. Sea coal was the chief cargo, with timber, stone and grain being carried on return. An intensive effort was made in the early 18th century to bring the heart of England in reach of its water-borne trade. Rivers were deepened whilst the flow of water was controlled by locks and sluices but by the 1760s, improvements in river navigation had reached an impasse. It was not until the building of the canals that a comprehensive transportation system linked the industrial north with the Irish Sea, with Manchester to the east and Liverpool to the west.

The Romans had constructed their famous Car Dyke which joined the cornlands of Cambridgeshire to the military garrison in Lincoln, and in 1560 the far-sighted city merchants of Exeter had built the remarkable Exeter Ship Canal. Still occasionally used by small ships, the canal starts in Exeter and, fed by the River Exe, pursues its own course for some 5½ miles down to rejoin the Exe Estuary near Topsham. But it was some two hundred years later before the Canal Mania, as it was known, transformed the industrial Midlands and the North. The Weaver Navigation Scheme was undertaken following the first Canal Act of 1755. It provided an outlet to the Mersey for salt mined in Central Cheshire. This was followed by the Sankey (1755–60) and the Bridgewater (1759–65) canals, constructed to serve the Lancashire coalfields with the result that the price of coal in Manchester was halved. In 1766 the most ambitious of canal schemes was begun. Conceived by Brindley, the intention was to provide continuous waterways from coast to coast. Called the Grand Trunk Canal, it was a 93 mile long canal cut from the Bridgewater Canal near Runcorn to a point on the River Trent from where it was navigable to the Humber Estuary. Brindley made this canal the basis of a comprehensive system of waterways linking England's major rivers and, in the process, brought a world market to Josiah Wedgwood at Etruria. As J. H. Plumb points out in *England in the 18th Century,* " . . . every canal cut cheapened goods, brought them within reach of humbler classes and raised their standard of living."

Built by inexpensive Irish labour, there was a network of some 2,500 miles of canals operating in England by the 1820s, and over 500 miles

Campbeltown on Fair Day, by McKinnon.
One of two planned towns established by the
Argyll family. The other town was Inveraray.

in Scotland and Ireland. Whilst these canals were clearly the basis for the prosperity of the Potteries, they also brought their own special kinds of buildings – wharfs, corn mills, inns and, of course, lock-keepers' cottages. At Stourport, in Hereford and Worcester, a whole new town was built in the mid-18th century around the basin that linked the Severn and Stour with James Brindley's canals. Canal buildings were functional and uniform. Cast iron was used for the window frames, while the openings in cottages and toll houses were standardised. The canal companies invariably used the same details and materials for all buildings.

Whilst the impact of the railway age in the 19th century was greater, the social significancce of the new canals was considerable. When the Oxford Canal reached Banbury from Coventry in March 1778, W. G. Hoskins points out. " . . . the church bells pealed all day, brass bands pumped away joyfully, and there was the usual civic dinner. Not least,

Lockkeeper's Cottage at Whixall, beside the Ellesmere Canal. The Canal was laid out by William Jessop in the late 18th century. The canalside buildings appear more as an adaption of the local vernacular.

the price of coal at Banbury Wharf came down to one shilling a hundred weight; and on the map of the local countryside there came to be marked numerous small roads called Coal Lane."

Fine complex of 18th century canalside buildings consisting of grain warehouse, inn and cottage at Stoke Bruerne, along the Grand Junction Canal. Converted to a Waterways Museum in 1963.

Materials for Building and Decoration

Many existing timber framed Tudor buildings in the more affluent south-east were either extended, or their casement windows were replaced by the latest sash window designs or the whole of a facade was re-fronted in the more fashionable style of the period.

The larger houses of the Tudor period in the south-east were invariably built of oak until the increased demand for oak by the shipbuilding and iron industries forced builders to use lighter and more economic timbers. The oak timbers of Tudor buildings were left exposed, the panelling between at first being wattle and daub, then later a replacement of brick nogging. But soon the economies in timber forced builders to find alternative means of covering even the frame itself. By the 18th century deal was increasingly used, covered by wood boards or hung with tiles or slate. The softwoods came primarily from Scandinavia and North America. In East Anglia the typical practice for hiding such economies externally was the use of a stucco cover to both frame and infill panels. These stucco walls were given a decorative finish known as pargetting, which is an ornamental design in relief in the plaster. It was fashionable in East Anglia between the 16th and 18th centuries and its origins are found in the more traditional incised work which takes the form of combed decoration. Floor joists were also used more economically, aided both structurally

Weather-boarded, timber frame houses at Tenterden, Kent.

Decorative plaster relief work at Rye, Sussex.

Timber frame cottage at Forden, Montgomeryshire. Characteristic is a lobby formed between entrance and gable fireplace.

Harehope, Peebleshire.
Small, early 18th century laird's house built of
harled walls with a yellow sandstone dressing to
the window openings.

Tile hanging, Rye, Sussex.

Porch on a mid 18th century cottage, Tenterden,
Kent.

and aesthetically by the now common practise of providing a lath and
plaster ceiling below. Many softwoods were imported for floor joists,
especially duing the Napoleonic Wars, which virtually doubled the
costs of building between 1790 and 1810.

With the exception of the very small house or cottage, brick was the
primary material used for house building by the 1770s. But the rising
cost of materials, coupled with the increasing demand for house
building, contributed to a general lowering of the standards in both
carpentry and bricklaying. Whereas, internally, economies in floor
joists were hidden behind plastered ceilings, externally, the elegant
shapes of many walls were nothing more than jerry-building, using a
soft and porous brick, frequently poorly laid. These economies were
obviated by the taste for smooth expanses of stucco as is the case with
John Nash's urban speculations, such as his Regents Park terraces.

In some of the expanding industrial towns, brick was used sparingly
because often the means of manufacturing brick locally was not
available, whilst transportation costs at this time were considerable.
The costs of using brick, however, were exacerbated further by the
imposition of the brick tax in 1784. This tax, not repealed until 1850,
was conceived as a means of raising money to cover the vast expenses
of the war in North America.

A result of the brick tax was the increasing use of brick tiles or
mathematical tiles. These brick tiles, designed to imitate bricks, are an
invention of the Georgian period. Never very cheap, they were
introduced originally as a rather expedient means of giving a more

fashionable appearance to the fronts of timber framed houses. With the introduction of the brick taxes, these tiles, which were not subject to the tax unlike the bricks they imitated, were an obvious alternative material. Found mainly in the south-east, especially the coastal districts of Kent and Sussex, these tiles were hung, or nailed like plain-tiling, to timber battens fixed between vertical studs. They were shaped in sections to give a brick-work appearance to the face. The illusion of brickwork was created skillfully with special corner tiles to maintain the bond, whilst their joints were bedded and pointed in mortar in the manner of brick walling. Headers and stretchers, as well as ribbed brickwork for window heads, were manufactured. Tell-tale signs of walling clad with mathematical tiles can be seen in the detailing around windows which only have a shallow reveal. First introduced to the south-east in the mid-18th century, mathematical tiles continued to be used for house building well into the 19th century. A characteristic of some of the seaside towns of the south-east is the manufacture of a version of the mathematical tile with a black-glazed face, by the turn of the century.

Junction of weather-boarding and stucco walls, Tenterden, Kent.

There is a complete absence of such tiles further north. A possible explanation is offered by Alec Clifton-Taylor in *The Pattern of English Building,* when he writes that "... there was something about this form of wall covering which was felt to be a trifle "fancy", even dishonest, that might have rendered it less acceptable in the North than in the more sophisticated – and at this time richer – South East." And in any event, what happened in house building in the more sophisticated Georgian heartlands of Kent and Sussex, would take some fifty to eighty years before making any noticeable appeareance in the Midlands or North, if at all. Because of rising costs in the use of such materials, timber framing became more popular, particularly for the housing of the poor, towards the end of the 18th century. Poorer, less susbstantial framing techniques were used to build many cottages and terraces, their frames rarely exposed. Instead of a cladding in brick tile, used primarily for the houses of the more well to do, oak or elm weatherboarding was used instead. By the early 19th century a preference developed in the counties of Kent and Sussex for cladding the frame with a variety of shaped tiles which had been moulded to create intricate and interesting patterns on walls.

Weather-boarding, Tenterden, Kent.

Utensils and implements had been made of cast iron up to the late 16th century, but with the denuding of the forests for the ship building and iron industry, coal was used as a fuel for the ironmasters' furnaces. But because of the sulphur content, the iron produced was too brittle and lacked the requisite strength. It was not until Abraham Darby, the ironmaster of Coalbrookdale, north-west of Ironbridge, discovered an alternative means of smelting iron in 1709, that it began to be used in great quantities again. It was he who first produced iron smelted by

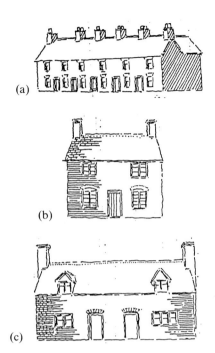

(a)

(b)

(c)

Ironbridge was the centre of English industrial life in the 18th century. The little hill town is built on a steep limestone ridge above a narrow gorge through which flows the River Severn. The dramatic Iron Bridge, from which the town gets its name, was designed and cast by Abraham Darby at his Coalbrookdale ironworks in 1778. The town has some good late 18th and early 19th century housing for industrial workers.
(a) Nos. 2-6 New Road, Ironbridge.
(b) No.1, St Lukes Road, Ironbridge.
(c) Nos. 14-15, Woodland's Road, Ironbridge.

Farmhouse at Newall with Clifton, North Yorkshire. The house was built of coursed rubble in 1737. The date is in an oval plaque above the entrance. To the left is a barn.

coked coal rather than charcoal. The Industry, once the pride of medieval Sussex, was moved wholesale to the Black Country of the Midlands, where large scale production was made possible. Here the raw materials, such as coal, iron ore, sand for moulding cast iron, clay for bricks and tiles and limestone to flux the slag in the blast furnacces, were readily available.

The Industry was further boosted by the invention of *Puddling* by Henry Cort in 1784. This was the method by which impurities in the molten iron, tending to produce brittleness, were reduced by means of stirring. It was Cort who linked the techniques of puddling and rolling into one continuous process for the manufacture of wrought iron. The puddling process was some 15 times faster than the more traditional method. By the mid-18th century, however, architects and decorators had found numerous uses for the material from staircase balustrading, balconies and fireplaces to elegant columns.

Before steel was produced in great quantities, most machinery was made from wrought iron. Only limited quantities of steel, which contains less carbon than cast iron but more than wrought iron, were available until the early 19th century. During the 17th and 18th century steel was made from wrought iron bars by the *Cementation process,* in which the bars were sealed in containers with charcoal and then heated to extreme temperatures until the iron was able to absorb some of the carbon given off from the charcoal. It wasn't until 1740 that an instrument-maker, Benjamin Huntsman of Sheffield, introduced into England the *crucible process,* by which small sections of cemented steel were re-melted in closed crucibles. The result was a high quality steel with a more even carbon content, a discovery that was to transform Sheffield into England's chief centre for high-quality steel production. It was here, in 1742, that Thomas Boulsover first developed the process of fusing silver and copper ingots and rolled the

Longfield House, Heptonstall, West Yorkshire.
Stone walled, double-pile house, built c.1730.

silver for which the city is famous. It was Joseph Hancock, in the 1750s, who was the first to develop the commercial potential of silver plating when he saw the possibility of silver plated table ware replacing the traditional pewter in the less affluent households.

Window glass was made in this country first by the Romans, and later re-introduced during the medieval period. Called *Cylinder glass,* it was made by collecting molten glass on to the end of a blowpipe and then blowing it into a sphere. The sphere, via twisting and turning the pipe, was then made into a long sausage shape. The ends were then cut off. The cylinder of glass was split open and then flattened out when cooled. The glazed panels were not very large, and it was not until the 18th century that larger sheets were made by what is known as the *crown method.* A more expensive manufacturing method, because of the wastage, it was made by blowing a ball of molten glass. An iron rod, known as a punty, was fixed to the centre of the base; the blowpipe was detached; the glass was reheated and the iron rod spun round until the hot ball of glass spun out into a flattish disc some 5 feet in diameter. The flatter central section of the disc was generally discarded for its poor quality, although some authorities believe it may have been used for glazing the windows of poorer houses.

43

No.41 Little Horton Green, Bradford, West Yorkshire.
Fine, stone-walled laithe house, built 1755. The barn is to the left of the house.

Knapped flint is a traditional material in the South-East. Lewes has several good examples.

Because of its expense, crown glass, which was marvellously transparent, was used primarily for glazing the sash windows of the larger mansions. For the smaller houses and terraces, cylinder glass was used. Improvements in the manufacture of cylinder glass in large sheets had been developed in Europe in the 18th century. But the large scale manufacture of window glass in Britain was not possible until the early 19th century because of the complex Window Tax. Introduced first in 1696, it was a levy on the number of openings in a house. The tax was increased on several occasions until reduced in 1825 and finally repealed in 1851. One result of the tax was the blocking up of many windows.

Cast Glass or plate glass eventually replaced cylinder glass and crown glass for glazing windows in the 19th century. First manufactured in England by Sir Robert Mansell in 1620, plate glass was made in the same way as cylinder glass, only in a greater thickness and of purer materials. It was an extremely expensive glass used chiefly as mirror glass or for the glazing of coach windows. It was the French who first developed a faster method of manufacturing plate glass by pouring molten glass onto a flat table where it was then rolled out. It was not until the late 18th century that this method was adopted on a large scale in England. Cast glass was used for window glass in England well into the 20th century.

One of the characteristics of Georgian interiors, especially during the Adam period, is the decorative use made of plasterwork with a variety of pattern reliefs made from standardised moulds. The boarded and beamed ceilings of the Tudor period were replaced by the decorative plaster ceilings in the Elizabethan period. Characteristic of Palladian houses was the application of stucco panelling to ceilings. By the late 18th century the fashion had changed in preference for low relief ornamentation characterised by a central decorative panel with light ornamentation between it and the encircling cornice and frieze.

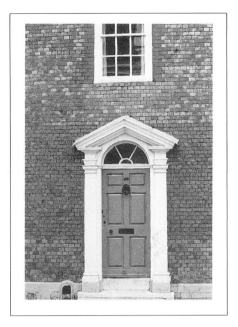

18th century house at the Western end of the High Street, Lewes, clad with mathematical tiles.

House in Abbey Close, Kelso, Roxburghshire. Built in the 18th century, of particular interest are the harled walls, exposed dressing and crow-stepped gables.

45

The practice of finishing walls in plaster, first employed by the Romans in Britain, was not re-introduced until the 17th century. The plastered walls were generally colour washed and sometimes gilded.

A variety of coloured marble was used in the grander mansions, not only for statuary, but also for decorative inlaid floors, ornamental chimney pieces and columns. A less expensive and more malleable material was *scagiola,* made of gypsum, glue and isinglass and stained, extraordinarily skillfully, to imitate marble. It was introduced from Italy and used in the late 17th and 18th centuries for columns and chimney pieces as well as for table tops.

18th century terraces, The High Street, Lewes.

Above left:

Ionic porch added in the early 19 century to St Anne's House, Lewes, a five bay, two storey house built in 1719.

Above:

Entrance porch to a Georgian town house, Lewes.

Left

Segmental arched porch, Lewes.

Windows

One of the marked characteristics of the smaller Georgian houses is their elegant sliding sash windows. They were far more expensive to install than the hinged wooden casements found in many cottages of the period, but the practical advantages, as well as the aesthetic distinctiveness of the sash window were considerable. By the mid-18th century the fashion-conscious owners of older timber frame houses were gradually replacing their leaded casements with sash windows. Such was the transformation that the cheaper wood casements were clearly identified with the vernacular tradition of the humble cottage, whilst the handsome sash windowed Georgian facades raised the standard of design of the smaller 18th century house to that of architecture.

Whilst sash windows are found in houses of the period in France, they are most characteristic of 17th century Dutch houses, and it was from Holland that the sliding sash window was first introduced into England. In Holland the tradition was for a smaller, fixed top sash with a longer, bottom sliding sash. In England the preference was for two sash windows of equal proportion.

The earliest English sash windows were rather cumbersome affairs, constructed out of large wood sections. Before the introduction of counterbalancing weights, the sash windows were kept open either by a series of pegs, inserted in notches cut in the grooves, or held by a series of hooks. When the counterbalancing weights, cords and pulleys were first introduced, the grooves were cut in the same massive wood sections as the window frames. Later the weights were accommodated in boxes forming part of the jamb resulting in a much lighter and more elegant window, whilst greatly economising in the use of timber. The first patent for sliding sash mechanisms used in England was taken out in 1774, whilst the patent for the first fastener, a barrel type with spring and screws, was granted in 1776.

The use of sash windows at Hampton Court, Kensington Palace and the Banqueting Hall, Whitehall was a great incentive for the rising middle class wishing to transform their houses into something more recognizably fashionable. But the practical advantages were also considerable in comparison with cumbersome casements characteristic of older houses. The taller window openings introduced by Inigo Jones in the Renaissance were of a size and shape eminently suitable for such a transformation, hence the scarcity of 17th century casements.

Georgian town house at Lewes, Sussex.

House in the High Street, Lewes, Sussex. A handsome five bay, three storey brick built house with a fine entry porch.

Above: **A Georgian house in the High Street, Shepton Mallet.**
There are a number of fine 18th century clothiers' houses in the town, such as Eden Grove and the Hollies. The town was an important wool centre from the 15th century.

Above right: **A house in the High Street, Lewes.**

Mostly the windows have equal sized sashes, but as architectural fashions changed, there was a preference for tall windows to articulate the principlal rooms, often on the first floor. These windows, generally running from floor to ceiling, were usually twice as high as they were wide and invariably gave access to a balcony. On the upper floors the windows were generally smaller. The proportional rule of thumb for windows of the smaller houses was for their height to be between one and a quarter and one and three-quarters times their breadth. The preference for more exaggeratedly tall windows belongs primarily to the Regency period.

The earliest glazing bars were invariably flat and heavy being cut out of solid wood. By the mid-18th century the glazing bars had become much thinner. In the Regency period many glazing bars were made of metal, whilst the thinner timber ones, often no more than ⅛th inch in thickness, required the fixing of glass to provide additional stiffening to the bars.

48

Building Legislation

The remarkable stylistic consistency of the brick-fronted, sash-windowed Georgian house is due, in part, to the architectural fashions of the time, but also to the design restrictions imposed by a series of building acts first introduced in London following the Great Fire of 1666.

Fire was the major hazard, with Roman London being destroyed twice, first in 61 AD and then again in 120 AD. There were further disastrous fires in 961 AD, 1077, 1087, in which St Paul's was destroyed, 1136 in which London Bridge was burnt, 1161, 1212 and 1264. The problem was not merely that of overcrowded London; other towns, most notably Canterbury, Chichester, Nottingham, Bury St Edmunds and Worcester, were also badly burnt.

The first building code in England was introduced in 1189 by Henry Fitz-Alwyn, the first Lord Mayor of London. Legislating for the thickness and height of party walls, as well as imposing minimum heights for jettied construction, it was designed primarily to reduce the risk of fire spreading from one building to the next.

There were further ordinances from 1212 onward prohibiting the construction in cities of certain fire hazards, such as ale-houses, in materials other than stone. Restrictions were also imposed on the use of certain fuels, whilst thatching was to be plastered or replaced by tiles or some other suitable material. Despite such legislation, control was difficult and most towns remained veritable fire hazards. Numerous decrees from the late 16th century had imposed restrictions on building in and around London, but with little success. In 1605 James I decreed that all new houses within the City were to be constructed of brick or stone, whilst no new houses were permitted to be built within a mile of the outside of the City boundary. But the demand for houses near London was such that, by 1619, James I issued another decree laying down more precise rules for both the planning and construction of such houses. It was important to control the expansion of major cities, such as London, as well as to reduce the danger of fire in the overcrowded city. Such restrictions proved of little effect and in the Great Fire of London, in September 1666, over 13,000 houses were destroyed.

The Act for the Rebuilding of the City of London, passed in February 1667, which catered for the re-alignment of roads as well as for the construction of fire-proof buildings, is the first comprehensive building regulation for London. This Act allowed for four distinct types of house. The first category consisted of smaller houses aligning

Chichester, Sussex. Handsome two and three storey Georgian houses in brick and stucco.

Elm Hill, Norwich, Norfolk.
A picturesque townscape of timber frame houses, typical of the 16th and 17th century.

School Hill House, No.33, The High Street, Lewes.
Built early 18th century, it is a five bay house with red dressings and grey headers.

House at Blandford Forum, Dorset.

minor streets and lanes. These were to be restricted to two storeys in height excluding cellars and attics. The second category, houses fronting more important streets and lanes, as well as the River Thames, were to be no more than three storeys high. The third category concerned houses aligning high streets and principal thoroughfares, which were not to exceed four storeys in height. The fourth category concerned the town houses and mansions of wealthy merchants and upper classes. These were generally large houses, standing in their own grounds. Like the third category, they were restricted to a maximum of four storeys. These larger houses were also required to have an external balcony at first floor level.

The Act foresaw the reconstruction of the City following the fire, with a series of more unified terraces, in both design and construction, aligning both sides of a street. Restrictions were imposed on the height of rooms, the structural thickness of party walls and external walls, the size of timbers for floors and roofs, and minimum distances were laid down for the proximity of timber to chimneys and flues. The regulations imposed by the Act, such as the fixing of the position of the ground floor to the street level as well as regulating the storey heights, were such that house designs quickly became standardised. The four house types were soon adopted throughout the country.

An important part of the act was the appointment of the first building surveyors. Without such control, a system still in use today, the jerry building and overcrowding of London preceeding the Great Fire would have been hard to avoid.

Additional acts included the imposition of a tax on every *chaldron* of sea-coal landed in London during the late 17th century, as a means of raising money for the rebuilding of the city churches and public buildings. In 1695 the Window Tax was introduced. It imposed a levy on all houses worth over £5 per annum as well as taxing each additional window in excess of a maximum six windows. This bizarre tax was increased on six separate occasions until it was finally repealed in 1851. To avoid excessive payment, many house owners had some windows blocked up, the blind windows being either of brick or sometimes stuccoed and painted as imitation windows. The blank windows were often there for reasons of symmetry and not always as a device for avoiding the window tax. These dummy windows are typical of the terraces in many of the spa towns.

Further legislation to reduce fire risks was introduced. In 1707 an Act banned the construction of overhanging eaves and cornices in London requiring, instead, that the walls be carried up as parapets to a height not less than 18″ above the roof. This Act also included specific arrangements for fire-fighting as well as prescribing the permissible dimensions for party walls. The most visible architectural affect of this particular Act was that the roof, quite a prominent architectural feature with decorative eaves and cornices, was now hidden by a parapet wall. In 1708 a further act specified the use of masonry or brickwork for the backs and jambs of chimneys not less than 9″ thick, whilst the flues were to be not less than 4½″ thick. Flues were to be ranged and the fireplace openings arched in brickwork. No timber was to be built within 5″ of a flue. In an attempt to stop the spread of fire via the windows of adjoining property a decree of June 1709 specified that no timber window or door frame in any new house should be positioned less than 4 inches from the front face of the outside wall.

In 1724 a building owner was required to give notice to adjoining owners of any intention to rebuild a party wall. In 1760 the actual thickness of the party wall was increased from 2 to 2½ bricks thick for cellars and from 1¼ to 2 bricks thick for the remaining storeys. The Act of 1764 banned the use of timber in the construction of hearths and increased from 5″ to 9″ the permissible minimum distance timber could be placed near a flue.

Until the Great Buildings Acts of 1774, previous acts had concentrated primarily on imposing standardization of bricks, restricting the use of timber on house fronts or legislating for the proper construction of party-walls. Many of the provisions are incorporated in our present Building Regulations, but it was the 1774 Acts, a milestone in the history of London 'improvements', as John Summerson points out in *Georgian London,* that was designed to consolidate and enforce the many provisions made in previous years. The Act was drafted by two of England's leading architects, Sir Robert Taylor and George Dance, the Younger. Sir Robert Taylor (1714–1788), described as 'the most successful architect of his time', was a Palladian at heart. The architect, amongst other things, of Heveningham Hall, Suffolk, he became surveyor to the Bank of England in 1765 and in 1769 was appointed Architect of the King's Work. George Dance, the Younger (1741–1825), whose design for Newgate Prison (1770–82) was one of the 18th century's great masterpieces, was the more innovative of the two. He was the son of George Dance, the Elder, architect of the Mansion House. He succeeded his father as Clerk of the City Works, London, in 1768.

The Act they drafted, as Summerson points out, was aimed at " . . . stopping once and for all the slipshod construction of party-walls and evasive quibbling between adjoining owners, and it aimed too at making the exterior of the ordinary house as nearly incombustible as possible." The Act legislated for the appointment of district surveyors to ensure construction was based on the provisions of the Act, as well as stipulating that a builder or building owner had to give 24 hours notice to the requisite authority prior to commencement of construction as well as detailing the work to be carried out.

Whilst the general principles of the Act were clear, it was felt

House at Chichester, Sussex. The county town of West Sussex, Chichester, the former 1st century Roman town, was a wealthy agricultural and commercial centre in the 18th century.

The High Street, Shepton Mallet.

51

Early 18th century three bay, three storey brick built house at Dorchester, Dorset.

necessary that, in order to deal more effectively with particular and special constructional and design problems, London buildings should be co-ordinated into a series of categories or 'rates', each 'rate' defined by particular building values and floor areas. There were seven 'rates' in total, six dealing with housing, the seventh with workshop building. The first 'rate' house, usually a three bay, four storey structure, was the most salubrious. Valued at over £850, it occupied nine 'squares of building' or some 900 square feet. The second 'rate' house was a narrower frontage house of two bays, but still four storeys high. The fourth rate house was only three storeys high with an even narrower two bay frontage. Valued at less than £150, it had a floor area of three and a half squares, or 350 square feet. The floor areas excluded ancillary accommodation. The fifth and sixth rates dealt with detached houses. Each "class" or 'rate' had its own code of structural requirements for the density of foundations, the thickness of external and party-walls as well as the positioning of windows in outside walls. One of the most important aspects of the Act was in the raising of the standards in the design and construction of speculative housing. The rating provided little room for variation, resulting in what later Georgians and early Victorians thought merely monotonous. However the Act did impose a minimum standard for working class urban housing.

By restricting the use of projecting cornices and exposed timber-work, as well as requiring windows to be concealed in brick reveals some 4″ deep, the Georgian house, with its various categories, became ubiquitous throughout the towns and cities of England. Such conformity and uniformity in the standard of housing was unusual in Europe. Whilst later generations of architects christened the Act, 'The Black Act' for its aesthetic rigidity, the originality in ornamentation at the time was such that it could cope well with the simpler, more austere buildings resulting from such constraints. It is perfectly clear, as Summerson has pointed out that " . . . in drafting the Act, Dance and Taylor – excellent artists both of them, as well as shrewd draftsmen – were thinking in terms of the most advanced types of London practice and merely crystallizing the regulations against this background."

Thr brick tax introduced in 1784 as a means of funding the fight against the American War of Independence, popularized tile hanging, an economic alternative and changed the character of many country towns in the South-East. But it was the London Building Acts of 1774, the last important building Act of 18th century England, that shaped the architectural form and character of middle class and lower class Georgian society. But whilst the anthropometric necessities were well catered for, the standards of hygiene were still deplorably low.

Terrace houses St Peter's Street, Chichester, Sussex. A flourishing wool centre in the 14th century resulting in many fine timber frame buildings. The handsome Georgian architecture is a product of the city's expanding clothing industry and wheat farming in the 18th century.

Public Health and Hygiene

Whilst the London Building Act of 1774 clearly raised the standard of both accommodation and construction of the typical Georgian house, there was little improvement in the public health and hygiene. In the mid-18th century the mortality in London was still very high. In 1764 there were 23,000 recorded deaths in London, of which 35% were of infants under two years of age. Few houses were connected with mains water supply and even less had any form of drainage. Most towns had open gutters for the disposal of household waste and S. S. Hellyer wrote in his book, *Plumbing,* published in 1873, that " . . . when people went into the streets at night it was necessary, to avoid disagreeable accidents from windows, that they should take with them a guide who, as he went along, called out with a loud voice, "Hand yer han." Most town houses at this time had a privy or closet erected over a cesspit in the back yard or garden. In the early 18th century these cesspits were emptied frequently by *nightmen* working with carts and buckets. The sewage, valuable to the early Georgian farmer, was carted out of town and sold. This soon proved uneconomical and communal cesspools or the nearby rivers were used instead. Many of these communal cesspools, generally badly built, leaked, often into nearby domestic wells causing fatal illnesses in many households. The use of rivers was hardly a preferable alternative since many, such as London's Fleet River (eventually to be covered in as a sewer in 1841) provided drinking water as well. In Edinburgh men were employed, Hellyer points out, to walk round the streets with pails swinging from a yoke carried over their shoulders. The pails had cloaks attached sufficiently large so as to cover the customer as well.

One of the crucial problems for any established community, has been the removal and disposal of human and domestic waste, as Jack Bowyer has pointed out in *The History of Building.* Since Neolithic man pits have been excavated for the disposal of refuse, but the primary system for the disposal of waste has been rivers and watercourses, fed, in the more advanced communities, by a network of open ditches and drainage channels. In the medieval monasteries, hygiene was considerably more advanced than in domestic practice, and the latrines, or 'necessarium' (necessary house) were generally flushed by rain water or by the waste from the main water supply. In many towns public *necessary houses* were often built out over a river or watercourse. Most of the larger medieval house's had cesspits, but these were badly ventilated and became extremely unhealthy in hot weather, contributing to the numerous outbreaks of epidemics.

Whilst attempts were made to control the growth and congetion of towns throughout the 16th, 17th and 18th centuries, sanitary conditions remained deplorable. Whilst floors were thoroughly scrubbed with soap and water, the Georgians washed themselves sparingly. Although domestic water was in short supply, bathing was still comparatively rare, most households washing themselves from small washstand basins. Portable copper baths were rare, and the only plumbed-in arrangement was a huge, 16' × 10' bath installed for George IV at the Royal Pavilion, Brighton. The use of wigs, powdering and cosmetics offset any dirt or odours, but with the decline of such fashions in the late 18th century, people began to take more care of their personal hygiene. De la Rochefoucauld, writing in *Melanges sur L'Angleterre* (c1784) describes, with horror, the low standard of cleanliness within the domestic kitchens: " . . . women are usually employed and are as black as coal; their arms bared too the elbow, are disgustingly dirty; to save time, they handle portions of the food with their hands . . . you will not see a couple of napkins or dish-cloths, and if you do see one in use, you will have no desire to wipe your hands on it." At this time clothes were washed in the house, no more than once a month, often taking some two or three days to do, including the ironing. The irons were usually of brass or steel with a wooden handle. To heat the iron a piece of hot metal was inserted from the rear into the base of the iron by opening a slide at the back of the iron.

It was not until the mid-18th century that London, and a few provincial cities, had a main water supply, all be it primitive. Only a few areas were connected, and what supply there was was intermittent. It was laid primarily to facilitate households connected to it to fill up their tanks for two to three hours a day for about three days per week. The principal sources of this piped water in London were the River Thames, Hampstead Pond and New River. None of this water was fit for drinking and, as Dr Lucas, writing in *An Essay on Waters* (1750), pointed out, the popularity of tea as a drink at this time was subscribed to the fact that the tea hid any unpleasant tastes remaining in the boiled water.

The planning of Georgian houses was made considerably easier without the need to accommodate bathrooms. Typical of the smaller Georgian house was the use of an outside privy, sometimes referred to as the *Jericho* or necessary house, placed at the bottom of the garden. It would have a wooden seat built over a cesspit. In some of the larger houses there would probably be a smaller seat, for the use of children so that they would not slip through the hole. The privy would usually be hidden from the view of the houses either by planting or by boarding, sometimes decoratively painted. Indeed, some households

had rather elegant timber or brick structures built resembling garden
temples. In some of the larger gardens it was not unknown, according
to John Woodforde, in *Georgian Houses for All,* for ladies, following
some appropriate excuse, to walk out into the garden and, under the
veil of a hooped skirt, to do what ever was necessary.

In houses of the more densely built sections of towns, privies were
often installed indoors with a cesspit dug below the level of the ground
floor. These cesspits were not always well managed and, when finally
finished with, were frequently forgotten creating numerous problems
later. Lawrence Wright in his book, *Clean and Decent* (1960), quotes
the story of a plumber in the late 19th century doing repairs beside a
kitchen sink under the light of a candle and being blown up by the
gases of a forgotten cesspit as he prised up the flagstone floor.

At night there were commodes in the bedrooms, whilst in most
dining rooms there was a set of chamber pots contained in a cupboard
or hidden behind curtains, placed there for, as Doreen Yarwood
points out in *The English Home* (1979), " . . . the relief of gentlemen
when drinking after dinner and after the ladies had retired into the
drawing room."

There were a few, rather crude water closets in existence in the early
18th century, but these were found only in the larger houses, such as
Kedleston Hall, Syon House or Osterley Park. There was generally
only one such convenience in such houses, usually installed in a

Early 19th century view of Queen Square, Bath.

convenient niche in one of the reception rooms. Rarely were such conveniences ventilated externally and the bad smells wafted through the house.

The first water closets in England were invented in the late 18th century, one of the earliest patents being granted to Alexander Cumming in 1775, with a patent for a slightly more sophisticated device being granted for an invention by Joseph Bramah two years later. There were numerous other versions produced in the 18th century, but all were expensive to install, limited in use and, because of the lack of adequate ventilation, unpleasant and sometimes dangerous. The most primitive one, which continued in use in one form or another until the late 19th century, was the pan closet. The pan closet consisted of an earthenware bowl resting on a hinged metal pan. The pan, contained in a mahogany casing, had a few inches of water in it when the bowl was level. To discharge the contents, a handle was pulled, the pan tipped down and the contents emptied into a cast iron receiver below, connected to a rudimentary drain. The problem with this system, however, was that it was impossible to empty completely the cast iron receiver, hence the likelihood of bad odours wafting up through the rest of the house. A later invention was the plunger closet, designed to stop the bad odours by means of a leather-faced plug which was lowered to close the outlet. The problem with this invention, however, was that the plug did not stay watertight for long.

Water closets were fitted into first and second 'rate' houses, but all other households had to make do with a privy opening into a cesspit emptied at night time. This state of affairs was not to improve until the development of public drainage systems in the late 19th century.

The Commissioners of Sewers and Pavements, in a report to the Lord Mayor, Alderman and Common Council of the City of London in 1765, pointed out that:

1. The pavements and streets of London are roughly paved due to the custom for householders to effect their own repairs to their frontages.
2. The centre channel provided is dangerous and disagreeble to foot passengers and carriages alike.
3. The common practice of depositing household refuse in the central channel of streets is dangerous to health.
4. The footways, not being raised above the street level, are often covered with mud.
5. Footways are obstructed with shop windows, showboards and cellar doors.
6. The increase in projecting signs to business and commercial premises obstructs the free circulation of air and intercepts the light of lamps.
7. Foot passengers are annoyed in wet weather by the discharge of water spouts from the roof.
8. Lack of street names and house numbers cause great inconvenience to strangers.

The contamination of water supplies by leaking communal cesspools was the cause of numerous cholera outbreaks. But whilst personal hygiene was deplorably low the establishment of quasi local authorities in the mid-18th century, coupled with an increasing concern for public cleanliness, did result in a significant reduction in the infant mortality rate. Between 1761 and 1765 several Private Acts of Parliament were secured by enterprising entrepreneurs enabling them to levy a rate on houses in return for the provision of a cleansing service.

By the late 18th century most major streets had common sewers, many of the diseases prevalent in the more congested urban centres had been checked and the birth rate began to pass that of the death rate. However, the drainage system, as such, was still only a pipe discharging into the nearest river. At the beginning of the 18th century, as J. H. Plumb has pointed out, " . . . the first noticeable thing about these towns would be the stench. There was no sanitary system; an open cesspool in the court often served the richer inhabitants; the poor . . . made a public convenience in every nook and cranny." By the late 18th century people still died from typhoid caused by poor water-

19th century view of Camden Crescent, Bath.

borne sewage arrangements, but the provision of better food, the treatment of water, the developments in medicine together with the foundation of hospitals and the removal of refuse from the streets resulted in a healthier, expanding population. However, the major improvements in the standards of public health did not take place until the mid-19th century until the passing of the Public Health Act in 1848, which established modern sanitary law and the appointment of the first public health surveyors with the Town Improvements Clauses Act of 1847, a provision later embodied in the Public Health Act of 1875.

Builder and Speculator

As John Summerson points out in *Georgian London* (1978). " . . . the speculative builder, the mainspring of London's expansion for three hundred years, had always been a person of the most various characteristics. Sometimes he has been a lord, sometimes little more than a labourer; sometimes a substantial capitalist, sometimes a craftsman, with only his skill and time to adventure; sometimes an architect, sometimes a bricklayer, a quack, an actor – indeed almost any class, trade or profession."

Nearly all the houses of Georgian London were speculative yet there were only a handful of building firms at the time. Most building craftsmen and labourers preferred to work freelance and for a major project, a man known as a master builder would be responsible for gathering together the tradesman needed.

Of building firms listed today as members of the National Federation of Building Trades Employers and established before or during the 18th century, one of the oldest is R. Durtnell & Son Ltd of Brasted, Kent, who were established in 1591. One of the earliest houses, Durtnalls at Pounds Bridge, Penshurst, built in 1593, still stands today as do a number of houses and terraced cottages built in the Sevenoak's area. Another survivor is W. B. Kingsbury and Sons Ltd, of Colchester, and Rice & Sons Ltd of Brighton, both established in 1620. The former firm prospered during the big middle class expansion of Colchester in the mid-18th century. Other survivors include George Tanner and P. O. Wicks Ltd, of Braintree, founded in 1700, R. Thornton & Sons, Skipton, 1727, Francis Newton Ltd, Hitchin, 1728, R. Vinall (Henfield) Ltd, Sussex, 1736, Asby and Horner Ltd, London, 1740, and William Anelay Ltd, York, 1747. The latter firm was established originally in Doncaster, where the founder, John Thompson had already been carrying out work for the Doncaster Corporation from as early as 1740. The son of a clockmaker, he worked as a bricklayer on the Doncaster Mansion House which was begun in 1744. The architect was James Paine, a Palladian, and contemporary of Sir Robert Taylor, and the man responsible for the design of Nostell Priory, Yorkshire (1733–50). Work on the Mansion House was delayed by quarrels with the corporation and by the Rising of the Young Pretender in 1745, when an army of 6000 were encamped on the Wheatley Hills.

The list continues with the establishment in 1770 of the firms of V. N. Still & Son of Southborough, Kent, and H. Hayward & Sons of

Laura Place, Bath. Designed by Thomas Baldwin in 1788. A small square, angled in plan, built for William Johnstone Pultney as part of his development of the Bathwick Estate.

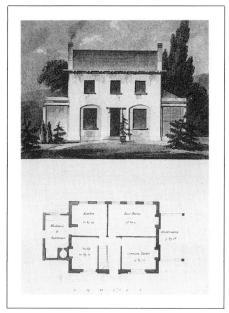

Illustrations from John Plaw's *Sketches for Country Houses*.
Published in 1800, the book contains designs for country houses, villas and rural dwellings designed for " ... persons of moderate income, and for comfortable retirement".

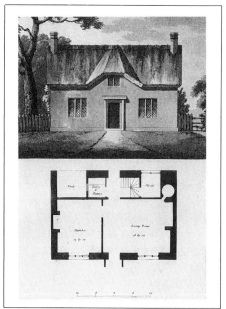

Saxmundham, Suffolk. In 1773 John Nicholls & Son of Wolverhampton was established; in 1774, Patching & Son Ltd of Brighton; 1775, C. G. Fry & Son of Doncaster; 1778, Trollope & Colls Ltd of London; 1780, Dove Brothers Ltd of London and W. J. Simms & Sons Ltd of Nottingham; 1784, A. M. Tomlinson Ltd of Leyland; 1786, Lovell Construction Ltd of Gerrards Cross; 1790, A. A. & R. J. Westmore of Newport, Isle of Wight; 1791, C. Ansell & Sons Ltd, Dorking; 1792, Watkin, Jones & Sons Ltd, Bangor; 1795, J. B. Abbot & Co. Ltd of London; 1797, Knowles & Son Ltd of Oxford and W. J. Mitchell & Son Ltd of London; 1799, Brazier & Son Ltd of Southampton and in 1800, the firm of R. Butcher & Son was established in Warminster, and Payne & Sons Ltd, in Swindon. Quite a good record when one remembers that for the builder and developer the risks were great. For the great landowner there was no risk, but the number of bankruptcies amongst Georgian builders was very high.

Many craftsmen, like John Thompson of Doncaster, combined the occasional speculation with contract repair work. Like some practices in the 1980s, especially housing projects in London Docklands, many projects were developed under a form of licence, in the sense that the builder himself did not pay for the freehold of the land. It was the purchaser who paid for it. The speculator would merely sign a building agreement with the landowner, taking out a lease for the land for between 60 and 90 years. For the first year only a peppercorn rent was charged. The speculator endeavoured to erect the shells of his house, advertised them with long leases and, would hope to complete a sale within the first year, thus avoiding the payment of ground rent. The purchaser, taking over the long lease as well, would then have the shells completed and decorated to his own family requirements. It was a system adopted for building in most towns of the period, and it is interesting to see a firm like Lovell Construction Limited, in their bicentennial year, still operating in a similar system in their housing projects with the London Docklands Development Corporation.

Most craftsmen were trained in a variety of crafts and were able to choose between being employed on a full time basis or of working independently. But to operate on his own such a craftsman had to become a kind of quasi-architect. However, the design of small terraced houses was made considerably easier with the publication of numerous pattern books of house designs of various sizes, styles and situations. Batty Langley testifies to the importance of such publications for the masons, carpenters and joiners of the building world, when he writes in his *The City and Country Workman's Treasury of Design* (1741) " . . . the great pleasure that builders and workmen of all kinds have of late years taken in the study of architecture; and the great advantages that have accrued to those for whom they have been

employed; by having their works executed in a much neater and more significant manner than was ever done in this Kingdom before; has been the real motive that induced me, to the compiling of this work, for their further improvement."

Whilst craftsmen working within the City of London were still controlled by the various companies, those working outside the city boundaries had no such restrictions. The London craftsman was, as a rule, as Summerson points out, " . . . a man of considerable skill and status – proud, conscientious and expensive. He lived well and drank heartily. He was capable of writing a fairly good letter and could usually (if he were a mason, bricklayer or carpenter) make a plain 'draught' of a small building."

The central figure in the building team was the master builder, but the key 'professional' was the surveyor. A descendent of the Tudor surveyor, he was responsible for the supervision of building work, estimating and pricing as well as making land surveys.

The title 'architect' was used by numerous people, although the profession, as we know it today, did not exist in England, as such, until the mid to late 18th century. Architects emerged from a whole range of backgrounds - Burlington was a landowner, Vanburgh and Archer, gentlemen of means, whilst others like Kent, a coach-painter, or Ripley, a carpenter, were recruited from the trades or ranks of surveyors. As Summerson points out "... the ability of the craftsman to better himself by becoming an architect or quasi-architect, provided a strong inducement to self education, even to the more commercially-minded man, for he could not afford to be behind in questions of taste. Self education meant getting a hold on the artistic needs of the centres of fashion. It meant the desertion of traditional craftsmanship and the adoption of certain academic formulas."

Above and below: Doorways in North Parade, Bath. Designed by John Wood the Elder in 1740, part of the architect's grandiose plans for this section of the City, of which only a handful of streets were built.

The commonest method of settling a contract was via a lump sum for the complete structure agreed with the master builder. Today's system of competitive tendering had not been conceived. Another method, thought to be a better way of controlling the quality of workmanship, was to agree sums for each trade. The skills of the master builder were usually limited to one of the key trades so that the other trades would have to be sub-contracted, and it was this system of sub-contracting that distinguished the Georgian building industry from that of previous centuries.

A great worry in the mid-18th century was that various economies forced on the building industry were resulting in technically ill-built structures. So widespread were such views that the London Building Acts of 1774 were concerned primarily with measures to make houses stronger, hence the ranking of such houses into a series of 'rates'. Whilst the act did have a marked effect in raising the general standard of building, it also resulted in a marked improvement in the architectural quality as well. New streets, because of the constraints imposed of size and height, were given a dignified and harmonious sense of conformity which makes this period of town building so memorable.

The working model for most speculators, was that of Nicholas Barbon, the late 17th century financier and businessman who, in a remarkably short period of time built numerous squares and streets of houses all over London. His standardised house types were designed to an economic minimum with all joinery and decorative elements based on repetitive patterns. Roger North in his *Autobiography*, published in 1887, pointed out that Barbon was the inventor " . . . of this new method of building by casting of ground into streets and small houses, and to augment their number with as little front as possible, and selling the ground to workmen by so much per front, and what he could not sell building himself. This has made ground rents high for the sake of mortgaging, and others following his steps have refined and improved upon it, and made a super foetation of houses about London." Member of Parliament as well as great economist, he was the first to initiate fire insurance, insuring over five and a half thousand houses between 1686 and 1692. But apart from his ingenious strategies employed in building speculation, he wrote a most important book, *The Discourse of Trade,* later to be quoted by Marx. Published in 1690, it set out to show the importance of building, both socially and economically, pointing out that building was 'the chiefest promoter of trade', since so many subsidiary trades were dependent upon it.

The lessons of Barbon were learnt well by the later Georgian speculators. One of the first phases of London building expansion in the early 18th century, a product of the peace and stability following the Treaty of Utrecht in 1713, was the development of the area

The Circus, Bath. Designed by John Wood the Elder, 1754-58.

Laura Place, Bath.

Old Palace Terrace, Richmond Green, Surrey. Marvellous group of six identical early 18th century terraced houses aligning the east side of The Green.

Henrietta Street, Bath. Designed by Thomas Baldwin in 1790 as part of the development of the Bathwick Estate.

Kings Mead Square, Bath. Designed by John Straham, contemporary of John Wood the Elder, in the 1720s. Straham, principally a Bristol architect, died c.1740.

between present day Regents Street west to Hyde Park, starting with two acres of land to the east with the development of Hanover Square and George Street by Lord Scarborough who had acquired the lease of the land. A contemporary development to the south, abutting Piccadilly, was the transformation of Burlington House and the setting out of a series of street to the rear for Lord Burlington, the great architectural patron of the Palladians such as William Kent and Colin Campbell.

These developments were followed by the layout of streets such as Bond Street, Conduit Street and Brook Street in the 1720s. The development of the Grosvenor Estate and the Cavendish-Harley Estate followed. For the latter development no less a talent than James Gibbs was employed to provide the architecture; Charles Bridgeman, the landscaping.

The expansion of London continued westward with the development of the Portman Estate beyond Marylebone Lane in the mid-18th century. Manchester Square was built in 1774 and work on the development of Portland Place to the north-east was started, followed by the development of the Bedford Estate. Work on the latter was carried out by James Burton, the most important and ambitious London builder since Barbon, as Summerson so clearly demonstrates, and who dominated the development of Bloomsbury until the early 19th century. In 1792 he took out an option for the whole of

Part of the New Town, from the North West, Edinburgh. Drawn by Thomas H. Shepherd.

Brunswick Square, built the north side of Bloomsbury Square, Burton Street and Crescent, and built the east side of Tavistock Square (demolished 1938). Like Barbon before him, he released many sites to smaller builders.

There were great opportunities for the building industry in the provincial towns and cities in the late 18th and early 19th centuries, despite a serious set back with the war in America begun in 1775, the financing of which was subsidised by the levying of a brick tax. There had been massive building work in Bath where the architects, John Wood, father and son, produced a series of magnificent terraces, a Circus and Crescent over a forty year period for several wealthy landowners. There was a large, middle class expansion of Colchester in the mid-18th century, whilst Cheltenham, another spa, rapidly expanded following a visit there by George III in 1788, which brought the town into the fashionable limelight. The interest of the Prince Regent in Brighton had an equally encouraging effect for the south coast Sussex town, and it was another enterprising builder, Thomas Kemp, who made his fortune in the building of a large estate to the east town, today known as Kemptown.

Whilst there were many enterprising builder/speculators in 18th century England, the most successful of all belongs to the period of Regency architecture and the great 'metropolitan improvements'. His name was Thomas Cubitt (1788–1856), a journeyman carpenter who had established a large workshop in the Gray's Inn road. With his stucco-fronted streets and squares, he completed what Burton began, and whilst Burton retired to the south coast to built St Leonards-on-Sea, Cubitt revolutionized the building world by employing for the first time all the necessary building trades on a permanent wage basis.

Terraces

The necessary constructional constraints for terrace design were imposed by the London Building Acts of 1774. The intention of the acts, as Dan Cruickshank points out in *Georgian Buildings,* was to "... consolidate, enforce and strengthen the provision for sound constructions enshrined in the 'previous acts, and apart from anything else it was very explicit about non-compliance. Work not executed in accordance with the act could be demolished or amended, and the workmen were liable to a fine of fifty shillings and to be 'committed to the house of correction'." The primary point of the act was fire prevention and secondly sound construction. The first was achieved by prohibiting the use of decorative wood as well as stipulating the setting back of sash windows, 4″ away from the front facade as well as on the concealment of the box behind the window jamb; the second was achieved by categorising permissible building types into a series of 'rates', of which the first four rates were concerned with terrace housing, the fifth and sixth with detached houses, and the seventh with industrial and agricultural building.

The need to comply with the conditions of the act meant the establishment of the principles underlying the form of terrace housing. The act also greatly encouraged the use of stucco and a new

The Circus, Bath.

Lansdown Crescent, Bath. Engraving by A. Woodroffe.

Devonshire Crescent, Buxton, Derbyshire. Designed by John Carr of York in 1780. Unlike the Circus, Bath, this is smaller, and semi-circular.

The Circus, Bath. Designed by John Wood the Elder, 1754. Stemming from an early idea of his for a "magnificent place for the Exhibition of Sports, to be called the Grand Circus", this was his masterpiece. Whether sports facilities were to be incorporated is doubtful but the remarkable theatrical facades were designed to evoke memories of Imperial Rome, with three tiers of Doric, Ionic and Corinthian columns. Of particular interest are the *grand,* formal to the Circus and the informal rear facade made up of accretions.

The Paragon, Blackheath, view from the communal garden.

composition, coadestone, for many architects of the period felt it was only by using such material that important buildings could be given the necessary enrichment. The strictures on design imposed by what some christened *The Black Act,* gave a mere brick facade what was thought to be a mean appearance. Stuccoing a facade certainly enriched it, it was believed. Some architects went further still, believing that certain terraces were important elements compositionally in the townscape and required to be more boldly articulated.

The earliest terrace houses of the period were a development of the single pile terrace house of the late 17th century. The typical terrace house was generally two rooms deep, three storeys high, with entrance, stair and passage along the party wall. Most had a semi-basement. This basic plan type was perfected in the hands of the Georgian builders.

Following the Great Fire, what remained of the gabled and jettied timber buildings was gradually replaced by those more regular brick built, narrow-fronted houses. In London all new houses, built following the Great Fire, were required to be of brick. These new terraces provided a uniform street composition, either of individual designs or as a repetitive unit in the overall composition.

The boom in brick building brought an inevitable shortage of skilled bricklayers. The result was that an Act of Parliament permitted London labourers to lay bricks without being members of the appropriate Guild. And one of the problems in the late 17th and early 18th centuries was that the more skilled workmen were often employed to erect the outer leaf only, whilst to economise the inner leaf was often built with rougher materials and workmanship. There was little or no keying in, resulting in the bulging walls of many house

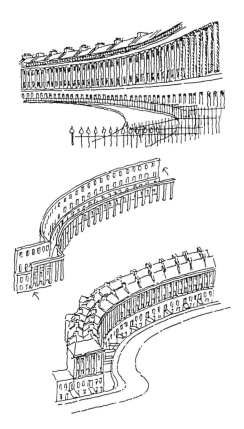

The Royal Crescent, Bath. One of the grand set pieces, not just of this City, but of European cities. Designed by John Wood the younger, 1767-75. A complete semi-ellipse, it is one of earliest English crescents, a dramatic facade of giant columns raised above a solid ground storey.

fronts. There was also a habit of using wood beams in the footings as well as bond timbers at various heights in the walls. This resulted in the settlement of some load-bearing walls, but serious cracks were often avoided because of the use of lime mortar which has sufficient give as to allow bricks to readjust in such situations, instead of breaking up.

A characteristic of the early 18th century was the astylar brick terraces such as Colin Campbell's design for Old Burlington Street, London (1715–1723). It is a handsome, brick terrace, austere and uniform in appearance, but proportioned according to Palladian principles. A contemporaneous strategy was the articulation of

Buildings around Queen Square, Bath.

terraces by a central pediment and flanking pavilions, such as Queen Square, Bath, designed by John Wood, the Elder in 1729. The latter, bedecked with the entablatures, columns and pediments of Roman temple architecture, was an entirely new, and redical urban compositional strategy in which a collection of terraces are given a palace front, for their principal, or public, facade. There are other interesting examples in Bath, such as The Circus (1754) by John Wood, the Elder or the Royal Crescent (1767) by John Wood, the Younger, as well as in cities and towns as far apart as Edinburgh, Buxton or Cheltenham. But, as Dan Cruickshank has pointed out, such monumental architecture outside of such cities, was largely beyond the pockets or ambitions of most developers

Towards the late 18th and early 19th centuries another strategy was evolved – a terrace in the form of a series of linked pavillions. Two good examples are Gloucester Circus, Greenwich (1790) and the Paragon, Blackheath (1793). Both by the architect Michael Searle, the former is composed of a series of brick built semi-detached houses, three storeys in height, their entrances in a lower, linking block. The main block is articulated by a ground storey of arched windows and a string course dividing the upper storeys with their rectangular windows. In the Paragon, Blackheath, a crescent of large villa blocks is linked by a single storey colonnaded pavilions. Such a strategy was developed further during the Regency period.

Architectural Pattern Books

The insanitary and dilapitated condition of cottages on many of the great estates in the 18th century was such that leading architects and writers of the day proposed numerous improvements. Batty Langley (1696–1741) produced over 20 books on architecture and building. A carpenter–surveyor, he produced numerous manuals on architecture and building construction as well as rather ambitious works such as *Ancient Architecture Restored and Improved by a Great Variety of Grand and Useful Designs.* Of particular interest is his *The City and Country Workman's Treasury of Design,* published in 1741.

A contemporary was William Halfpenny, (d. 1755) who described himself on the title page of one of his books as "architect and carpenter". He published many manuals for builders as well as collections of designs for farmhouses and cottages. The most notable of his books are *Rural Architecture in the Gothic Taste,* 1752 and *Rural Architecture in the Chinese Taste,* 1750–55.

William Pain (1730–1790) was another English architect to style himself "architect and carpenter". He published many manuals of architecture and building between 1763 and 1786, including *The Builders Treasure* and *Builders General Assistant.* His most popular book was *The Practical House Carpenter,* published in 1789. This latter book contained clear instructions for Georgian carpenters to follow, including heights of pediments, methods for calculating their pitch, etc.

In *Hints to Gentlemen of Landed Property,* published in 1775, Nathaniel Kent produced a set of practical plans for cottages, stating that " . . . all that is required is a warm, confortable, plain room for the poor inhabitants to eat their morsel in, an oven to bake their bread in, a little receptacle for their small beer and provisions and two wholesome lodging apartments, one for the man and his wife and another for his children". The plans included dimensions as well as an estimate of costs. But it was John Wood, the architect of the Royal Crescent. Bath, who was the first to publish a pattern book devoted entirely to the housing of workers. In his *Series of Plans for Cottages of Habitations of the Labourer,* published in 1781, John Wood describes in detail the practical and aesthetic requirements of such cottage design, suggesting that cottages ought to be built in pairs so that " . . . the inhabitants may be of assistance to each other in case of sickness or any other accident". He also held strong views about the positioning of windows, urging people to " . . . let the window of the main room receive its light from the East or the South; then it will

Illustration from John Plaw's *Sketches for Country Houses,* showing the design for a cottage or small farmhouse. It was designed to be built of cob construction for a site in the New Forest, Hampshire.

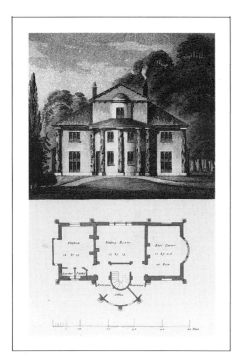

Illustration from John Plaw's *Sketches for Country Houses.* House designed for an artist. The site is again in Hampshire.

always be warm and cheerful". He also suggested that each cottage should have a privy – a facility rare even in the farmhouses of the day.

Whilst the mid-18th century was concerned more with the practicalities of such cottage construction, the predeliction in the late 18th century was for the overtly picturesque. Variety in aesthetic effect became of crucial importance with the result that cottages were built with irregular walls, projecting eaves, gabled ends and porches with elaborate barge boards over their gabled roofs. William Halfpenny was certainly the first to extol the virtues of such picturesque irregularity; the cult was firmly established by Sir Uvedale Price's *Essays on the Picturesque,* published in 1794. This was followed by such books as James Malton's *Essay on British Cottage Architecture,* published in 1798, and intended to demonstrate how builders could conserve the vernacular tradition, a way of building which, he suggested, was the effect of chance.

Price maintained that " . . . there is, indeed, no scene where such variety of forms and embellishments may be introduced at so small an expense, and without anything fantastic or unnatural, as that of a village; none where the cover of painting and the cover of humanity may find so many sources of amusement and interest." And the characteristic properties of village architecture, as distinct from that of the city, " . . . are intricacy, variety and play of outline."

The concept of landscape as an extension of architecture, which epitomised the design of the early to mid 18th century country mansion was gradually replaced by the preference for an architecture conceived as a related and picturesque part of the landscape.

Illustration from John Plaw's *Sketches for Country Houses.* **Design for a Gothic style cottage. The columns supporting the roof overhang are trunks of trees.**

Illustration from Atkinson's *Views of Picturesque Cottages.* The book, published in 1805, contains plans for labourers' cottages and small farmhouses, as well as providing information on the different materials used for building them.

In *Hints for Dwellings,* published in 1801, David Laing produced the designs for a series of thatched roofed octagonal and hexagonal cottages, " . . . for particular situations in which the regularities of the surrounding scenery had been attended to." The late 18th century preoccupations with the cottage ornée resulted in numerous lodges and gamekeepers' cottages with decoratively thatched roofs, projecting eaves and ornamental barge boards. But it was not until the early 19th century that a whole village was built according to picturesque principles. This was Blaise Hamlet, in Avon, built in 1810–12 by John Nash for the Quaker banker, J. S. Harford. Each of the nine cottages, wrapped around an irregular curving village green, is varied in plan and style with exaggerated roofs, deep, overhanging eaves and decorative chimneys.

There were still those who preferred the more rational and common sense to the picturesque solution for rehousing the labourers on an estate. John Plaw in *Ferme Ornee or Rural Improvements,* published in 1795, made many practical suggestions as to the ideal schedule of accommodation, developed further in the plans presented to the Board of Agriculture by Robert Beatson in 1797, in which a variety of cottage types were depicted.

Whilst, as Nathaniel Kent pointed out, many landowners still spent more money on the construction of their stables and kennels than on decent housing for their labourers, there were, however, notable exceptions, seen at their most vivid in the model towns and villages built on a few of the great estates. And it was such pattern books that helped shape and form such settlements.

Cottage designed by John Nash at Blaise Hamlet near Westbury-on-Trym, Avon.
The cottages, for old retainers of the client, Mr. Harford, are of the most varied character, arranged in a picturesque layout around a village green.

Another new house type, to be developed more thoroughly during the Regency and Victorian periods, was also introduced – the villa. The suburban villa, described by Clive Azlet and Alan Powers *The English House,* as the first truly middle-class house type, was a fashionable, but compact residence. In 1793 Charles Middleton outlined three types of villas in *Picturesque Views for Cottage, Farm Houses and Country Villas.* The first was " ... the occasional and temporary retreats of the nobility and persons of fortune from what may be called their town residence. Secondly, as the country houses of wealthy citizens and persons in official stations, which cannot be far removed from the capital: and thirdly, the smaller kind of provincial edifices, considered either as hunting seats, or the habitations of country gentlemen of moderate fortune. Elegance, compactness and convenience are the characteristics of such buildings ... in contradiction to the magnificence and extensive range of the county seats of nobility and opulent gentry." The first category is represented by Palladian recreations such as Chiswick House, Mereworth Castle and Marble Hill; the second category by the handsome villas of Robert Taylor or Sir William Chambers such as Asquil House, Richmond 1761-4 or Duddingstone, Edinburgh, 1762; the third category, which was epitomised by speculative middle-class Victorian developments, was first outlined in 1794 in a plan for Eyre Estate in St John's Wood. The remarkable thing about this project, as Sir John Summerson has pointed out in *Georgian London,* " ... is that the whole development consists of pairs of semi-detached houses. So far as I know, this is the first recorded scheme of its kind – a kind which was to become almost universal for suburban development in the later 19th century and which remains almost universal today."

Model Villages

Traditional cottage, near East Stratton, Hampshire.

The traditional 'open villages' were a product of centuries of gradual development and growth, self-contained and localised within parishes and manors, and it was here that vernacular building was largely developed. The shape of such building was determined by the particular use; the level of technological expertise provided the necessary form and space; the availability of building materials provided the possibilities for style.

But the architectural style and character of the village itself were shaped by a complex series of factors as diverse as the building types with which the village itself was composed. The major influencing factor was the very nature of the village itself. There were feudal villages such as Penshurst and Chilham, in Kent, or Audley End, in Essex, where the whole way of life was bound up with that of the great mansion or Hall. The village almshouses and schools were usually provided by the local lord, as were the cottages and shops. Throughout were the tell-tale signs of such authority – the coat of arms on the inn, gates and monumental boundary walls of the great house, family memorials and chapels in the church – each detail symbolic of the feudal emsemble of served and servant.

In other villages, growing up in the shadow of great religious

Cottages at East Stratton.
The village, designed by George Dance c.1800, consists of five pairs of estate cottages, modelled on the traditional vernacular cottages of this area of Hampshire.

Milton Abbas.

Milton Abbas. The model village built by Lord Dorchester in the late 18th century to the design of Chambers.

establishments, both building and daily life went hand in hand with religious observance. Abbeys and priorys were the major architectural set pieces. Schools, hospitals, inns, mills and workers' cottages, all the elements associated with both their business and charity work as well as those neccesary to sustain everyday monastic life, grew up around them.

The most marked changes to the building and architectural character of the traditional village occur with the agrarian and industrial revolutions of the 18th century. The enclosures of the 18th century, reshaping the fields into the pattern we know today, resulted in larger, more compact farms. Under the system of strip-farming, the farmhouses and cottages were grouped within the village, for building outside the old village boundaries was restricted by the complicated ownership and rights of the strip. The abandonment of the ancestral village by the bigger farmers meant that the village farmhouse was now divided into two or more cottages to house the farm labourer.

Further changes occurred with the development of a distinct architectural style that transcended the vernacular tradition typical of the older villages of the period. The handsome brick built sash windowed houses of the Georgian period made a considerable impact on the character of the village. Numerous timber-framed houses in the village street were also refronted in the fashionable style of the time by owners unable, or unwilling, to afford a new building. Such refronting consisted either of a simple brick facade only or the addition of a one room deep addition along the whole of the front of a house.

The typical villages are those grouped around greens, often spacious, straddling the junction of winding routes or aligning one long street. In the 18th century a strategy for a more formal village was developed. This model village, or closed village, was a product of 'emparking' or the need to accommodate an expanding agricultural force or to house an industrial community. Such villages were the creation of the landowning classes. Under the ownership of one man, they were a product of a particular vision, social or architectural, designed not by local builders but by architects.

One of the earliest of the model villages is that of Chippenham, Cambridgeshire. It consisted of a series of colour-washed, semi-detached cottages built c1700 outside the gates to Lord Orford's country mansion. The one and a half storey high cottages are linked by single storey out buildings. These cottages replaced a number of earlier cottages demolished to allow for improvements to the existing house and park. It allowed for the tenants, employed by the estate, to be housed nearby. Although such ideas for 'emparking' had been mooted before, (the landscaped plans for Castle Howard, proposed in 1699, included a small village), it was the first to be realised. Others soon followed. The village of Well Vale, Lincolnshire was rebuilt from 1725 as a product of emparking; New Houghton was rebuilt along an avenue by Sir Robert Walpole in 1729 outside the gates to Houghton Hall; at Gayhurst, in Buckinghamshire, 16 houses and an inn were repositioned by George Wright along a main road between 1738 and 1739; Kedleston in Derbyshire was rebuilt to make way for the rerouting of the turnpike following an Act of Parliament in 1760, and in 1764 the whitewashed terraced cottages of Audley End were rebuilt by Lord Braybrooke outside the gates to his magnificent Jacobean mansion.

There were many others, of course, but the most celebrated are the villages of Nuneham Courtney, in Oxfordshire, and Milton Abbas, in

Chippenham, Cambridgeshire. Built at the beginning of the 18th century, this was one of the earliest model villages. The semi-detached cottages, linked by single storey outbuildings, have bedrooms in the roof lit by dormer windows.

The Walks, Groombridge.
A row of 18th century terraced cottages built at the top of the village green. The ground storey is of red and blue brick, the upper storey is tile hung.

Nuneham Courtney. Model village rebuilt in the 1760s. It consists of one and a half storey high, brick built pairs of cottages aligning the Oxford Road. Nuneham is thought to have been the 'Sweet Auburn' of Oliver Goldsmith's 'Deserted Village' (1770).

Dorset. Nuneham Courtney, thought to have been the village celebrated in Oliver Goldsmith's famous poem, *The Deserted Village,* replaced an original village swept away by the Earl of Harcourt intent on creating a classical landscape as seen from his house, a vista in which the existing village intruded. Rebuilt in the 1760s, the 19 semi-detached cottages, minister's house, inn and forge, are a Georgian style version of the local vernacular tradition. The model village of Milton Abbas was rebuilt by the Earl of Dorchester to replace a small market town removed because it spoiled his view. The model village, masterminded by Capability Brown and William Chambers, was begun in 1773 and consists of a series of identical semi-detached cottages set back behind a stretch of lawn aligning a winding, sloping village street. Work on the village was completed in 1786.

A number of small hamlets were extended or rebuilt during this period of 'improvements' and new estate villages planned. Examples include Bradmore, Nottinghamshire, an estate village built by Sir Thomas Parkyns in the early 18th century; Ormiston, East Lothian, another early 18th century village established as a market centre for the estates of the agricultural pioneer, John Cockburn (1679–1758); Capheaton, Northumberland, a model village built (from 1752) by the Earl of Crewe from the ruins of the Abbey, and stone cottages with Tudor details flanking the gates of Ripley Castle, Yorkshire, erected between 1780 and 1860. The most formal of all these new estate villages was that of Lowther Village, near Askham, Cumbria. Designed by the Adam brothers between 1765 and 1773, the village consists of a series of two storey terraces, austerely classical in design, built of a rose-coloured stone. The terraces are laid out around a semi-circle, the only built section of what was intended to be a classical

76

circus, opening axially onto a square planned in the form of a cross.

Such improvements were often no more than a handful of cottages added to an existing village, such as East Stratton in Hampshire. Built by George Dance for Francis Baring in 1806, the village consists of nine pairs of 2 storey high, brick built, thatch roofed cottages with entrances in gabled porches, inserted in single storey outshuts aligning the sides of each pair. Goerge Dance based the design of his cottage on the vernacular tradition of the area.

A number of new villages were conceived as self-contained settlements. Fulneck, Yorkshire, one of the first of the Moravian Settlements to be built in Britain, was founded in 1748, complete with chapel, housing and school. Like Fairfield, in Lancashire, founded in 1785, it managed to sustain, as Gillian Darley points out, "... a relatively self-sufficient economy which, though religious in origin (the Moravians being a non-conformist sect originating from Northern Europe) was not authoritarian or repressive".

Model village. Designed by John Carr of York, around the gates of Harewood House, Yorkshire in the 1760s. Series of grand, stone-built terraces, varied in scale and articulated with the elegance one expected of the smaller urban terraces of the period.

There were numerous model villages planned for the industrial centres too. Examples are Portreath, Cornwall, a small port with pier and cottages founded by Francis Basset in the mid-18th century to cater for the tin industry; Abbeydale Hamlet, near Sheffield, an industrial community established by Earl Fitzwilliam in 1785; Morriston, Monmouthshire, beginnings of what was intended to be a sizeable town, laid out to house colliery and copper workers from 1768 onwards; the pink stone built mill village of Cartrine, Ayrshire, founded by Claud Alexander and David Dale from 1787 onwards; and the handsome mill village of Marple, Cheshire, built by Samuel Oldknow in 1770. Also in Cheshire is the village of Styal, a remarkable survival of the industrial age, consisting of a series of cottages, two chapels and apprentice house built by Samuel Greg, a Belfast man, from 1784 onwards. The village was established to house the workers for the cotton mill he established in an idyllic wooded valley of the River Bollin. Because his employees came some distance, he first converted existing buildings on the site to house them and then, as the business expanded, built the first of a series of new cottages.

One of the most pioneering of these early mill villages was that of the cotton-milling village of New Lanark, Lanarkshire. Founded by David Dale in 1783, it consisted of a series of terraced tenements with accommodation for 1000, planned around four mills. In 1800 Robert Owen, the son-in-law of David Dale, took over the management. David Dale also founded another cotton-spinning mill village at Blantyre, Lanarkshire in 1785, this time in association with Richard Arkwright, the pioneer of mechanical cotton-spinning. It was here, incidentally, that David Livingstone, the missionary and explorer, was born in 1813.

There were also a number of interesting canal villages and sea ports

Traditional thatched roofed cottage, Hampshire.

constructed during this period. One of the earliest is Buckler's Hard, Hampshire, established originally as a port by the Duke of Montagu to capitalize on the trade with his West Indian sugar plantations. Planned along a bank of the Beaulieu River, it was built from 1727 onwards and consists of a single wide street and spacious lawn lined with a row of handsome red brick Georgian houses. The spa town and quayside at Mistley, Essex, was planned by Richard Rigby from 1768 onwards with some of the work buildings being designed by Robert Adam. Wedgwood established a potteries village and factory called Etruria, near Burslem in Staffordshire. Built along the banks of the Trent and Mersey it was opened in 1769. Apart from a row of cottages little is left of what was once described thus in Warner's *Tour through the Northern Counties of England* (1802) " . . . a long uniform, and neat village, inhabited entirely by the workmen of Mr Wedgwood, introduced us to the manufactory, which is as picturesque as a building of this kind can well be; the Staffordshire canal here resembling a river, rolling its waters between it and the elegant mansion of Mr W., the banks shaded with trees, and rising beautifully on each side. Here upwards of 200 people are employed." The classical style of architecture established at Etruria became the norm for such enclaves throughout the potteries. Another interesting canal village is that of Shardlow, Derbyshire. Complete with carrier's houses, yards and warehouses, it was built from 1777 onwards as a canal port and terminal following the opening of the Trent and Mersey Canal. Of particular interest is the stone built Broughton House, a handsome carrier's house built in 1800, in a commanding position overlooking yard and basin, with a curved verandah crowning its entrance porch.

Another town that owes its existence to the coming of the canals is Stourport, built round a basin linking Brindley's Canal to the River Severn. Of particular interest is the long, red brick Georgian warehouse and the architectural elegance of the Tontine Hotel, opened by the canal company in 1788.

In Ireland there is an especially fine canal-side village of Robertstown, Co Kildare, with a handsome 3 storey late 18th century hotel, a long row of terraced two storey whitewashed cottages, and a spacious quayside complete with installations and a fine canal bridge.

The Georgian Interior

The streets and squares of Georgian England are fine indeed. Some, especially those of the fashionable spa towns, such as Bath or Brighton, are of a sumptuous scale and decorative richness that only the wealthier and more enlightened speculators were prepared to pay for. More typical are the town houses designed to a calculated minimum permissible under the various Building Acts of the 18th century.

Nicholas Barbon, the late 17th century speculative builder, was the first to see the enormous potential in the mass-production of housing. The houses making up the numerous squares and streets that he built are all very much alike, as Summerson points out " . . . economically planned to the point of meanness, with coarse ornaments which repeated themselves over and over again. The design of the panelling and staircases of his houses never varies, and his carpenters must have turned out thousands upon thousands of the twisted balusters whose slick modernity was calculated to engage the eye of the bumpkin in search of his first town house."

He was the model for the later Georgian speculator, many of whom had standards far lower, in both construction and design, and it was not until the London Building Acts of 1774, that an acceptable minimum standard was enforceable. The remarkable degree of uniformity and conformity of the Georgian street was a product of this Act, which prescribed heights and sizes for a variety of house types, and created a spacious and dignified townscape. But behind the public face, the standard house interiors were comparatively compact. Whilst a first rate house had a floor area of 900 square feet, a fourth rate house had a floor area of only 350 square feet. Not surprisingly, the rooms in such terraces are comparatively modest – 12 feet × 12 feet to probably not much more than 15 feet square. Such compact planning had considerable effect on both the design and positioning of furniture, as engravings of the early 18th century testify, depicting furniture pushed up against the walls, with only the dado rail saving the wall surface from damage. It was considered important to give as much free space in the centre of a room as was possible. It was only during the late 18th century and early 19th centuries that furniture began to encroach on the centre of the rooms, the chairs, tables and sofas arranged in a comparatively casual manner.

Mahogany longcase clock, c.1780.

Early 18th century mahogany side table.

79

Early 18th century settee.

Mid 18th century quadruple chair back settee

Living Rooms

In the larger mansions and town houses of the early 18th century, it was typical to find, as in their Palladian precedents, the principal reception rooms arranged symmetrically about the first floor, the piano nobile. These houses were usually three storeys in height, often with an attic storey. In the smaller country houses, generally two storeys in height, the principal rooms are on the ground floor.

In the early part of the century, comfort and convenience were less prized than splendour, and spaciousness, so that whilst the main rooms occupied the best part of the house, servants quarters were squeezed into attics, whilst the kitchen, larder and scullery were relegated to the basement or, as in some of the country mansions, incorporated in an outbuilding. Whilst there were obvious disadvantages to such inconvenient planning of kitchens, the problems for the larger households was mitigated somewhat by the great quantity of servants on hand.

The drawing room was generally lavishly decorated. The typical room of the period would have an encircling cornice, and panelled wainscot. The wainscot was painted, and the wall above generally covered in wallpaper.

The fireplace, positioned centrally along the wall, usually the gable end, would have richly carved marble, or painted and gilded wood or stucco surrounds. In the early 17th century the traditional open hearth had a cast iron fireback. A detached firebasket was later used, raised

Mahagany sofa with serpentine back, late 18th century.

Fireplace wall of the King's Room, Traquair House.

up on dogs, or legs, to create a better draught. This was known as a dog-grate. A characteristic of the Georgian period, was the basket-grate. In this design the dogs were made an integral part of the fire-basket which also incorporated the solid, cast iron fireback. Many fine designs were produced, based on the decorative and architectural patterns currently in fashion.

Another item was the fire screen, known as a pole screen. Characteristic of 18th and early 19th century reception rooms, the pole screen consists of a mahogany screen, circular or rectangular in shape and decorated with either a painted or embroidery design. The screen was fixed to a central pole and stand.

The caryatids of classical Greek Architecture, the support in the form of a sculptured female figure, the most famous example being the six figures supporting the south porch of the Trechtheion on the Acropolis, Athens, reappear in late Georgian architecture. In the domestic world they are found as supports to the chimney pieces in some of the grander houses.

A particularly fashionable feature was the decoratively carved pinewood chimney-glass. This was a gilt framed mirror attached to the chimney breast above the mantelpiece. The decorative details of such rooms were carefully co-ordinated, so that the panelled doors and windows would have appropriately carved and gilded pediment and mouldings. In the principal ground floor rooms opening onto gardens, or those on the piano nobile, giving access to balconies, the sash windows reached from the floor to the cornice level. Elsewhere windows were contained in a band between wainscot level and cornice. The windows would have damask or velvet curtains gathered in loops. Walls were adorned with pictures and ornate wall mirrors. Under most mirrors were side-tables or consoles. The console table, usually with a heavily gilt marble top, was designed to stand against a wall as it had only two supporting legs, additional support being provided by the wall. Another characteristic piece of wall furniture of the late 17th and early 18th centuries is the pier table and pier glass. Positioned on the wall between windows, hence pier, the pier table is a delicately carved, usually semi-circular table supported on four, slender legs. It is generally crowned by a pier glass, fixed to the wall, and consisting of a tall central panel with smaller and lower flanking panels.

The availability of larger sheets of glass resulted in a number of architects using mirror to create an illusion of spaciousness, especially in smaller houses. These mirrors were designed as an integral part of the interior architecture. In the early 18th century, mirrors generally had a carved and gilt pinewood frame, designed not unlike a door or window frame, and crowned with a pediment. A characteristic of the mid-18th century were decorative rococo mirrors of carved and gilt pinewood with candleholders. Smaller versions, called girandole, were

Mid 18th century mirror with carved pine frame.

Giltwood pier-glass, c.1765.

An early 18th century mirror.

Good example of 18th century panelling.

Kneehole desk.

Kneehole writing table.

Early Georgian walnut bureau.

designed as decorative wall brackets for candle fittings with a small mirror backing.

The 18th century was the golden age of furniture design in England. The classical style governed the design of most every day objects. Little was ugly, and all of it was the latest and most modern, especially the furniture design. Rooms were, on the whole, sparsely furnished, and the selection of furniture careful, for the major criteria was in the creation of an appropriate setting. All furniture was new, for it was not the practice to incorporate antiques with *modern* furniture. The names associated with 18th century furniture design include famous architects such as William Kent and Robert Adam, or Chippendale, Sheraton and Hepplewhite, the celebrated cabinet-makers of the Georgian period.

The concern for good craftsmanship, especially where it was to be on show, extended to the quality of joinery detail for doors and architraves, as François de la Rochefoucauld pointed out during a visit to Bury St Edmunds in 1784. He particularly liked the doors for they "... are always smooth and shut firmly... the key is always beautifully made. The chairs and tables are made of mahogany of fine quality and have a brilliant polish like that of finely-tempered steel".

A characteristic of the larger mansions and town houses until the 1760s, were doors flanked by pilasters or columns and crowned by a pediment. The preference under the influence of the Adam brothers from the late 1770s, was for a more straightforward doorcase with decorative frieze and crowning cornice. In the more affluent household, panelled doors of polished mahogany were typical, each panel decorated with a brass or ormolu ornamental relief.

During the reign of James I there had been a preference for rather heavy, boldly articulated, oak furniture. In the Georgian period furniture was extremely light and delicate in design, the primary items found in reception rooms being chairs, tables, sofas and occasional stools. The compactness of many plans meant that most cupboards were built-in or were designed as slim, wall-mounted units with glazed doors or, like the bureau-bookcase or bureau-cabinets designed, with pull out writing desk with drawers or cupboards, to stand up against a wall. Numerous woods were used, but when the heavy import duty on mahogany was lifted in 1721, it became increasingly popular in furniture design, eventually replacing that of walnut, which was easily perishable. Mahogany was available in broader planks, was easier to carve, did not crack or warp, and was extremely strong and worm-resistant. The pie-crust table, a round table with raised scalloped edge and fashionable from the mid-18th century, was generally made of mahogany. The Pembroke table was also made in mahogany or in set in wood with painted or veneered decorative work. It had slim, tapering legs with a drawer and side flaps which formed a rectangular or oval top when open, supported by hinged or sliding brackets, and ws popularised by Hepplewhite and Sheraton from the 1770s.

Marquetry as well as the use of brass inlay, both characteristic decorative techniques of the 17th century, were revived. Marquetry

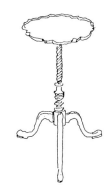

Mahogany tripod table.

Mahogany Canterbury.

Mahogany Pembroke table.

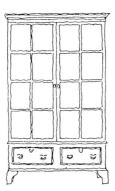

Mahogany bookcase.

Late 18th century secretaire bookcase.

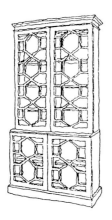

Mahogany bookcase.

techniques had improved considerably by the early 18th century so that it was possible to cut woods such as walnut, maple or yew in sheets as thin as $\frac{1}{16}$th of an inch. It was then possible to glue these larger sheets to a basic frame. Instead of utilizing the decorative marquetry patterns exploiting different woods, characteristic of the 17th century, simpler geometrical patterns, using the same wood, but exploiting the variety and direction of grains, became fashionable. The summit of Georgian veneer work is in the late 18th century furniture designs of Hepplewhite and Sheraton. Painted satinwood or mahogany furniture was especially popular from the late 1760s. The designs were either floral or festoon patterns contained in panels, or allegorical scenes, again framed in panels and sometimes painted by more celebrated artists.

In the early Georgian period, floors were generally of polished wood for carpets were very expensive at this time. When the Huguenot carpet weavers fled France to escape religious persecution following the Revocation of the Edict of Nantes by Louis XIV in 1685, many settled in England. With the help of Royal patronage, they were able to re-establish their craft by the mid-18th century, in towns such as Wilton and Axminster. In the early 18th century many carpets were still imported. Mainly oriental and costly, they were rarely found outside of the larger houses, and even in those they were not large, covering only the centre of the principal reception rooms. By the 1750s many fine English carpets were being produced. Carpets from the east, especially from Turkey and Persia, were imported in considerable quantities, as well as fine French carpets. In the later 18th century, some architects, like Robert Adam, had carpets made up to their own designs so as to echo the design of the ceilings above. Good examples are those made for Syon House and Osterley Park. It was rare to carpet stairs until the early 19th century.

Ceilings were generally plastered. In the Palladian houses ceilings were generally given a ribbed pattern. In the later 18th century, the influence of Robert Adam, with his preference for a pattern of low relief consisting of a decorative centre pieces connected by ornamental loops to a classical cornice and frieze was considerable. The ornaments were generally white or gilded with pastel coloured backgrounds of pale blues, greens, pink or cream, etc. Ceilings became less ornate towards the turn of the century.

In *Essay Towards a Description of Bath,* published in 1749, John Wood, the Senior, gives a marvellous description of house interiors of the period: "...floors laid with finest clean deals, or Dutch oak boards; the rooms were all wainscotted and painted in a costly and handsome manner; marble slabs, and even chimney pieces, became common; the doors in general were not only made thick and substantial, but they had the best sort of brass lock put on them;

84

walnut tree chairs, some with leather, and some with damask or worked bottoms supplied the place of such as were seated with canes or rushes; the oak tables and chests of drawers were exchanged, the former for such as were made of mahogany, the latter for such as were made either with the same wood, or with walnut tree; handsome glasses were added to the dressing tables, nor did the proper chimneys or peers of any of the rooms long remain without framed mirrors of no inconsiderable size; and the furniture of every chief chimney were composed of a brass fender, with tongs, poker and shovel agreeable to it."

In the early 18th century, most walls were covered in carved pinewood or cedar panelling, the lower section wainscotted in oak. By the 1720s onward, it was usual to paint the panelling in pastel colours or white. The carved decorative work was sometimes gilded. Decorative stucco work was a more fashionable alternative between 1720s to the 1760s. Panelling or stuccoing was generally applied to the walls of principal reception rooms, halls and staircases. In bedrooms the practice was to hang a covering of velvet or silk between cornice and dado rail.

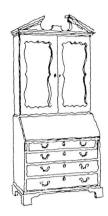

Mahogany bureau cabinet.

Whilst stucco had been the cheapest and earliest method of covering the walls of reception rooms in the early 18th century, its continued popularity from the mid-18th century onwards was due almost entirely to the decorative inventiveness of the Adam brothers.

Wallpaper, first imported from China in the late 17th century, was another alternative. It was then extremely expensive, but was seen as a necessary background for the Oriental porcelain and furniture, then fashionable to collect. The papers were in small sheets, but by the 1740s sheets as wide as 4 feet, usually containing a print depicting a garden or landscape, were imported. The earliest English wallpapers at this time were of painted or stencilled patterns in imitation of the velvet or silk hangings. Gradually wallpapers became less expensive and more readily available in this country. In 1754 John B. Jackson established a factory in Battersea to produce printed wallpapers. The first designs were imitations of Chinese wallpapers, but soon papers with overall floral patterns or landscapes imitating those of Claude Lorrain, Poussin or Canaletto were being printed. These papers were mounted on canvas stretched on a wood frame. The manufacture of wallpaper in long strips was produced first in France in the 1760s. It was not until the turn of the century that long strips were readily available in this country. Although the fashion was to cover all the wall, from dado rail to cornice level, people were quite happy to put up with the numerous joins which were inevitable when using the smaller sheets of wallpaper then produced.

Early 18th century kneehole bookcase.

The larger houses would have a principal saloon and possibly a private sitting room as well as a library. In the smaller houses it was the

Mahogany bureau bookcase.

Oak side table, early 18th century.

Mahogany dumb waiter.

Mahogany wine cooler.

practice to have a dining room and drawing room, but in the larger farmhouses the family would live and eat in the parlour. In the cottage the main room was the kitchen, although some might have a parlour attached. The furnishings for farmhouses and cottages were altogether more rudimentary. A characteristic feature was the Windsor chair. These stick-back chairs were made by the turners and wheelwrights of the village from the early 18th century onwards. The earliest design was the comb-back chair, named so because, with its shaped top rail and stick back, it looks like a hay rake. From the mid-18th century onwards, the bow-backed Windsor chair was a characteristic feature in farmhouse parlours and kitchens. In this design the back is arched in a continuous piece of wood. A decoratively carved plank forms the spine for the backs of both chair designs.

Dining Rooms

In the typical terraced town houses of the period, dining rooms, as numerous engravings testify, were comparatively congested. Whilst the detailing of doors, windows and fireplaces was similar to that in the other reception room or rooms of the house, the furnishing of the dining room and decoration of the walls were altogether less elaborate and ornate. There was a sideboard or sideboard table placed against a wall, as is the custom still, on which were stood the plates and silver. Such tables had been in use since the 17th century. Robert Adam designed a table in the 1760s, with flanking pedestals containing store cupboards. One pedestal was used as a plate warmer, the other as a cellaret, which was generally a metal-lined cupboard used for the storage of wines in the dining room. Urns were stood on each pedestal. In one was iced drinking water; in the other was hot water for washing up the silver. Most cellarets were large, free standing mahogany buckets, often octagonal in shape and raised on legs with casters to stand about 2 feet high. Again they would be metal-lined. Cutlery was generally kept in a Knife Box. They were decorative containers, shaped often like urns, and made in pairs to stand on sideboards. They were used from the late 17th century onwards.

The sideboard replaced the traditional dresser in the more affluent households. The dresser, with its drawers, cupboards and shelves, was removed to the kitchen. In the humbler farmhouses and cottages it was still, however, an essential item of furniture in the parlour throughout the 19th and into the 20th century.

An important article of dining room furniture was the dumb waiter. Invented in the late 18th century, it consisted of a tier of circular trays, generally two or three, attached to a central pedestal supported on a tripod base. Placed near the host or hostess, it was used to carry plates

Queen Anne chair.

Late 18th century dining chair.

Dining chair, c 1770.

Late 18th century dining chair.

of food, or bottles of wine and glasses. Equally important was the mahogany canterbury. Of the same period, it was used in dining rooms to carry cutlery and plates or, in the drawing room or library, books and papers. It consists of a table top in two divisions encircled by miniature stick balustrading to stop articles falling off. The top is carried on four angled legs.

There were also china cabinets with glazed doors, carved and gilded candlesticks and, most important of all, a polished mahogany dining table and matching chairs.

87

Wine cooler.

Mahogany breakfast table, c. 1780.

Welsh dresser.

The 18th century was a period of overeating and overdrinking. Throughout the century, breakfast, generally eaten fairly late, about 9.30 to 10 am, was comparatively light, consisting of rolls and butter or bread and butter, tea or chocolate. Lunch, eaten around midday, was merely a snack. The main meal of the day was taken later at 2 to 3 pm. In the more affluent households this meal was somewhat later still and by the late 18th century it was not begun much before 5 pm. In the early part of the century there was often a light supper around 6 or 7 pm, although not everybody took it. By the late 18th century the great length of the main meal, together with its later start, should have made such a supper unnecessary, but such traditions die hard. Much meat, of various kinds, was eaten together with vegetables, apparently badly cooked, baked puddings and jellies as well as large quantities of fruit. The wealthy drank spirits, home-made liqueurs and imported wines. Soft drinks were popular, as was tea and coffee. By the late 18th century, it was fashionable for the wealthy to take afternoon tea. As a consequence, the principal meal of the day was eaten later.

Until the high taxation and increased cost of living, towards the close of the century, as a result of the Napoleonic Wars, the poor ate comparatively well. There was plenty of meat, bread, home-produced cheese, vegetables and ale. In the poorer households, where cooking facilities were inadequate and fuel scarce, the norm was a meal of bread, cheese and beer.

Kitchens

As has already been pointed out, the larger farmhouses had spacious kitchens where the family sat and ate. It was the same for the humble cottager, for his kitchen, as such, was his principal and probably only room. Bed alcoves beside the fire were not uncommon. Some cottages still had only earth floors which were sometimes covered with rushes. In the larger houses, the kitchens were either in basements, attached to parlours, or in an outbuilding. They were often inconveniently planned in relation to the dining room, food having to be carried up stairs or along lengthy corridors. The ready supply of servants in the household made such inconvenient planning less of a problem. But it was necessary to have plate warmers and other devices to keep the food hot on arrival in the dining room.

The servants, garretted in the attics of the great house, ate their meals in its kitchen. It was also here that the poorer traveller for whom the house provided hospitality would take his meals. The early 18th century kitchens were fairly large, with stone floors and plain plaster walls. There was an open fireplace with a chimney crane hinged to one side. The crane had an arm on which pans and kettles were hung. There was a spit for roasting meat with a dripping tin, a rectangular metal tray, below to catch the fat. To one side of the fire was a circular brick oven for baking. Everything was cooked over the fire. Cakes were cooked on a girdle; whole fish were cooked in oblong or oval-shaped metal fish kettles. The kettle had handles at both ends, a lid, and a raised pieced bottom on which the fish was laid. When cooked, the fish was lifted out on the piece of metal bottom by attaching long handles to each end. There have been elaborate toasting devices, apart from the traditional fork, used since the middle ages for toasting meat, cheese or bread. There were several manufactured during the 18th century, including a standing toaster complete with adjustable prongs, and a down-hearth toaster consisting of a flat tray with four hoops to hold the bread or meat, the tray raised on legs. It was laid flat on the hearth beside the fire.

There was a shallow, stone sink, filled by cold water carried in buckets from a pump outside. The dresser, once a feature of early 18th century dining rooms, was adapted with shelves to take kitchen utensils, whilst the cupboards below were used to store linen. In order to keep food fresh, large quantities of salt were required, stored in a wooden salt box; costly spices, needed for flavouring the food were kept in a wooden spice cabinet, consisting of a series of interlocking compartments. The cabinets were locked.

Salted ham and bacon were hung from the ceiling beams, along with herbs and strings of onions. Milk churning, butter-making and preserving were carried out in the house. Candles and soap were also home-made.

There were numerous technical innovations for the kitchen. In the mid-18th century a smoke jack, used for turning a spit was invented. This jack, attached to the end of the spit, had a vane rising at right angles to it into the shaft of the fire. As the hot air rose, it turned the vane and finally the spit. At about the same time, a cast iron hob-grate was manufactured. The fire grate was flanked by iron hobs on which kettles and pans could be kept hot. Flanking the fireplaces were built-in wall cupboards used for warming plates and drinks. By the late 18th century, the first of the kitchen ranges, which revolutionised cooking, had been invented.

Life was considerably more primitive for the cottager. In medieval cottages a larger hood sometimes projected in front of the fireplace to catch the smoke. This was replaced when the whole chimney breast was brought forward. Many fireplace openings were six feet or more in width and the hearth was usually raised. An adjustable swinging arm pot crane, rather more primitive than those of the grander houses, allowed for several hanging pots. The convenience of the cooking fireplace later replaced open-fire cooking. To one side of the fireplace

Windsor chair.

Windsor armchair, c 1750.

Bow-back Windsor chair.

Comb-back Windsor chair.

Mahogany tester bed.

Mahogany tester bed

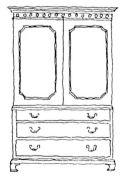

Mahogany linen press.

would be the bake-oven which was usually hollowed out in the thickness of the wall or built projecting on the outside.

Bedrooms

In the early 18th century it was rare to carpet bedrooms, even in the larger houses, and the bare floor boards made the bedrooms draughty. Most bedrooms were provided with brass or steel firegrates.

The rooms themselves were sparsely furnished, the principal items of furniture being the curtained four-poster. Such beds, referred to by John Woodforde as a "room within a room", were designed to counteract the cold. It was not only the wealthy who possessed such beds, four-posters were also common in the more modest 18th century households. In principle, the four-post bed consisted of a wooden framework of posts, head and canopy, covered in fabric. The earlier four-post beds were covered in heavy velvets and damask, but those were gradually replaced by floral or strip-patterned silks.

The early beds were rather high, necessitating a short flight of steps in order to climb into the bed. By the mid-18th century these beds became lower, the curtains less bulky and gradually more and more of the timber framework was revealed.

The tester, or canopy, was supported by the bedhead abutting the wall and two columns at the front. As more of the timber work was revealed, the more decorative it became. A frieze and cornice in the classical manner were incorporated during this period.

The internal furnishings of the four-post bed consisted of sheets and a large feather quilt on a springless base. A variation of the four-post bed was the tent bed which, like its name implies, looked like a tent when the curtains were drawn. Like the four-poster, the main object was to keep out the draughts from the bare boarded floors. But unlike the four-poster, it was generally much narrower, rarely accommodating more than one person. The hangings were fixed to an iron frame. They were cheaper to make and were generally seen in the more humble houses. Quite plain and straightforward looking were couch beds. They had headboards and footboards. There was also a rolled cushion, similar to that on the couches seen in some private sitting rooms. In the early 18th century it was not uncommon to find houses in the more primitive regions, such as the single storey crofters' houses of Northern Scotland, with a bed recess built within the thickness of the wall. The floor of the house was usually of unbeaten earth. In Orkney many beds were accommodated in small projecting alcoves, while on the mainland, timber box beds were common in the 18th and early 19th centuries.

Cleanliness was a problem; bed bugs were rife, especially in the more affluent houses causing Madame Johnson, in *The Young Woman's Companion* (1765), to suggest that people " . . . set open the windows of the bedchambers and uncover the beds to sweeten them; which will be a great help against bugs and fleas . . . spurge with a mixture of spirits of wine, spirit of turpentine and camphire."

The cleanliness of houses was a matter of some concern. In *Cottage Regulations*, issued by James Burton, the builder, in 1831, there were recommendations for the preservation of health. When the great Georgian builder retired from London, he set about the establishment of a small seaside resort, St Leonards. As J. Manwaring Baines of the Hastings Museum has pointed out he was " . . . not content with building houses, it was typical of the man that he should endeavour to improve the lot of those who might live in them." The *Cottage Regulations* included " . . . such suggestions as regular washing of floors, opening of windows, removal of refuse and even personal items of clothing and diet." Some firms specialised as bug-destroyers. The beds of many Georgian inns were in such a state that some travellers took the precaution of carrying their own bed linen.

For centuries the principal method of washing was via small washbasins in the bedroom. In the early 18th century it was rare for people to bath regularly. When they did it would have been in a round or oval hip bath, with a high back. There were soap containers or trays on the sides. Some had hinged lids. The bath would be hand-filled, and in the humbler houses, where hot water was scarce, the bath was usually placed beside the kitchen fire. The slipper bath, or boot bath as it is sometimes called, for it is a boot-shaped, metal bath leaving only the head and shoulders of the bather uncovered, was designed specifically for family baths beside the kitchen fireside.

The early Georgians had a ewer and basin provided for washing. You could do little more than rinse yourself. The basin stood on a chest or cabinet. There was room on the stand for the paints and powders, used by both men and women, as well as the strong smelling essences. The latter were used to ameliorate the smells incurred through the habit of people rinsing themselves only, in preference to taking a regular bath. The washbasin was replaced in the mid-18th century by a washstand, consisting of earthenware or porcelain basins with cabinet below containing small drawers and shelves. A gentleman's bedroom would have a shaving-table, complete with basin, drawers, compartments for shaving equipment and mirror with magnifying lenses. The table was so designed that the gentleman could sit and shave.

Most bedrooms had a night commode or pot cupboard. Pot cupboards, sometimes known as night cupboards, were kept beside the bed. They consisted of a simple earthenware or porcelain pot kept

Late 18th century bedside cabinet.

Early 18th century mahogany armchair.

Mahogany washstand.

Night commode.

Mahogany tallboy.

Oak secretaire table.

in a cupboard until needed. The commode, found mainly in the larger houses, was a grander type of chest of drawers which, when the top was opened, revealed a pot beneath the lid. The pot was called the chamber. Earthenware was preferred to metal, and by the mid-18th century colourful, ornamental porcelain pots were being produced from the Potteries.

Other items of furniture in the bedroom were a tall boy, a two tiered chest of drawers introduced in the early 18th century and a hanging wardrobe, introduced towards the end of the century and designed specifically to hang clothes in, especially ladies' dresses. Previously, such wardrobes only had drawers, as in the tall boy which it eventually replaced. The custom for wig wearing resulted in the manufacture of wig blocks and wig stands for the bedroom. The wig block was made in wood and leather and stood on a small circular table top carried on a tripod or pedestal base. Some stands had drawers containing materials for wig-dressing. The wig stand was generally kept beside the bed. The wig block and stand were in use from the late 17th until the early 19th century.

Many fine dressing tables were manufactured during the late 18th century. Ornately decorated, generally with marquetry, they were either variations of the knee-hole bureau with side cupboards, drawers and mirror, or more decorative tables carried on four slender legs. The table itself might be surmounted by drawers carrying pedestal-like cupboards acting as supports to an elegant, hinged mirror. Made in mahogany or satinwood, the variations are countless. The first purpose-designed dressing tables had been introduced first in the late 17th century.

Lighting

The primary source of lighting at night was candlelight, rushlight or lanterns. The well-to-do bought good quality candles which, in the larger houses, would be fixed in elaborate chandeliers. There were also various sconces, candelabra and wall-mounted girandoles with bracketed candleholders and gilded mirrors to reflect the candlelight. In the less well off households, candles were home-made.

The 18th century candles did not provide as good a quality of light as our 20th century candles. The fat of tallow candles burned quicker than the wick, smoked excessively and gave off a bad odour. They also needed constant trimming. Beeswax candles smelt less, gave a brighter light, but were very expensive. Most who could afford them, bought a comparatively inexpensive candle, know as dips, which were sold in bundles tied by their wicks. More expensive were candles made of a mixture of tallow, sperm whale oil, and coconut oil. But because of the glycerine content, these candles burnt poorly. It was not until the invention of the popular star candles by a French chemist in 1831, in which the glycerine had been removed, that there was a marked improvement in the quality of night time illumination. In the early part of the 18th century fewer lights were used; by the late 18th century, the major improvements were in the variety and number of lights used. In draughty spots, such as entrance halls or porches, covered lanterns were used.

The poor were unable to afford candles, even home-made ones. Their source of light were rushes dipped in mutton fat. Rushlight had been used since Roman times. The rushes, inserted into an iron holder, could burn for up to an hour. Gilbert White in his *Natural History of Selbourne* (1775), calculated that one pound of rushes would provide 800 hours of light for a cottager in the countryside. But in the countryside people used such facilities sparingly, choosing instead to regulate their lives according to the daylight hours.

The early chandeliers were of carved wood or ormolu, but as early as 1714 glass chandeliers were being advertised for sale. Designed with cut-glass drops, they were commonly called lustres. By the mid 18th century there was a flourishing trade in glass lighting equipment, rivalling that of the expanding pottery industry. It was also possible at this time to buy a peg lamp which burned whale oil, but gave off much smoke. By the late 18th and early 19th centuries, oil lamps which burnt colza seed oil were readily available. These early oil lamps had a clockwork pump to assist the flow of oil onto the wick.

There had been numerous experiments in the 18th century on the production and use of coal gas. But it was a Scot, William Murdoch, who founded the commercial coal industry. He had used gas generated from coal to light the rooms of his house in Redruth in 1792, and when he moved to Boulton and Watt's Soho factory in Birmingham, he lit the factory with gas produced in retorts fed by 15 lbs of coal contained in iron pots. Further gas lighting installations were made by Boulton and Watt for various companies in and around the Manchester area from 1806 onwards. But it was a German professor, who, on arriving in England at the turn of the century demonstrated the use of gas by the lighting installation he made for the Lyceum Theatre. Changing his name on arrival in England from Albrecht Winzer to Frederick Winsor, he soon realised that the one-off installations by Boulton and Watt were impractical in the long term and that gas would have to be piped under the streets from large, central gasworks. He attempted to form a National Light and Heat Company in 1806, but the company failed to get the necessary Government Charter. In 1807, however, he lit the south side of the Pall Mall with gas piped from his house and, in 1812, a more modest version of his original proposals, the Gas Light and Coke Company received its Charter. 1815 was the year in which, according to J. H. Plumb, " . . . Great Britain seemed on the edge of bankruptcy and social revolution. Starvation was driving the poor to wreck the machinery which seemed to them to be the cause of the misery, and the government, without wisdom and without foresight, repressed brutally what in its turn it could not comprehend." By December of that year 26 miles of gas mains had been installed in the City of Westminster.

Until 1805, when matches similar to those of today were invented, the best way of lighting fires and candles was by means of tinder and flint. The process consisted of striking a block of flint downwards, with the serrated edge of a piece of steel, onto some tinder, generally cotton cloth. It was some time before a spark would set the tinder to smoulder. The smouldering tinder was then used to light a pinewood splinter which had previously been dipped in sulphur. The candles and fires were then lit by this pinewood match.

The first matches to be manufactured were called bottle matches. Invented in 1805, they consisted of splinters of wood coated with a mixture of potash, sugar, gum and sulphur. To light them you dipped them into a bottle of concentrated sulphuric acid, hence their name. Lucifer matches, the first of the friction matches to light by being struck against a sandpaper surface, were invented in 1829 by John Walker, a Durham chemist. He sold his matches from his chemist shop in Stockton-on-Tees for a couple of years, leaving others to develop his idea. It was not until the mid 19th century that a Swedish firm developed the idea of coating one of the outsides of a matchbox with a form of phosphorus against which a match, stored inside the box, would be struck. These were the first of the safety matches which we know today.

Heating

The Romans had developed a fairly sophisticated heating system. It was an indirect heating system consisting of the construction of hypocausts, or heating chambers, laid under the ground floor of their villas. A flue linked these chambers to a fire chamber built in the external wall. The concrete floors were raised up some 2 feet high on pillars of clay tiles. The flue gases would heat the concrete floor, its thermal capacity keeping the temperature in the room at an appropriately comfortable level. In the bath building at Aquae Sulis, present day Bath, hollow clay voussoir blocks were used to heat the vaulted ceiling, whilst Roman flue tiles were used for heating walls.

Anglo-Saxon Britain, following the withdrawal of the Roman

Bolection - moulded fireplace of the early 18th century with a lugged surround.

Legions, reverted to the old, primitive method of heating – an open hearth. Although the Great Houses already had chimneys by the end of the mid-fifteenth century, the smaller houses and cottages seldom had chimneys before the reign of Elizabeth I. The cottage fire was still laid in the centre of the room on the bare earth floor, the smoke escaping as best it could. Later a hole was made in the roof. But the

95

Dressing room fireplace with flanking pilasters and panelling of the early 18th century. The grey marble chimney-piece was installed in the mid 18th century.

ever present danger of fire in the Middle Ages made the brick chimney a necessity.

Coal fuel had been used in the London breweries and bakehouses following the Act of 1212 which forbade the use of straw as a fuel in such buildings. The increasing use of coal was such that in the Act for the rebuilding of the City of London following the Great Fire, a coal tax was imposed. But the principal fuels in towns and cities throughout the 17th century was wood and charcoal. In the early 18th century, coal was the principal fuel in London, but it was expensive and of such poor quality that it created a dense, black smoke.

Gradual improvements had been made in fireplace design over the centuries. The coal grate was introduced and Sir Hugh Plat had suggested that, in order to increase the draught, the hearth should be narrowed and the throat made smaller. Much of the heat from such fires was still lost up the flue. In early 17th century Paris a system had been devised by which air in the room was drawn under the level of the hearth, warmed as it circulated in ducts behind the fireplace and back, through grilles in the mantlepiece, to the room again. The use of metal canopies of hoods built out over the grate, as well as free-standing stoves, was a French invention in the early 18th century. Unlike the funnel of lathe and plaster hoods of the smaller houses of 16th and 17th century England, there was a valve to restrict the amount of air and heat escaping up the chimney, whilst convection currents of warmed air were created within the room by the heat of the metal canopy. These fires were never popular in England.

Smoking fireplaces were a continual problem. The critical dimension was the distance between the size of the hearth, and the distance from the top of the fire and the flue throat. In the late 18th century fire openings were made smaller, and most grates were coal burning. The traditional open fire, as Robin Barry has pointed out in *The Construction of Buildings* (1979), " . . . consists of a great inset in a fireplace recess formed in a brick chimneybreast . . . As its name implies an open fire is clearly visible and this is tis chief attraction. The disadvantage of an open fire is that much of the air drawn into the fire and up the chimney by convection is not necessary for combustion or burning the fuel and this excess air wastefully takes a large proportion of the heat from the fire into the chimney. The air drawn into the fire is replaced by air drawn into the room which causes draughts of cool air which are uncomfortable and wasteful of heat. An open fire inset in a recess in a chimney built into an external wall will lose some heat to the outside."

One of the characteristics of Georgian chimneys was the addition of chimney pots. Although they had been used in France before the 18th century, they were rare in England.

Chimney pots were popularised under the reign of George III, but it was the Victorians who introduced their use on a large scale. They were introduced as a device for reducing the smoking of fires by increasing the draught in the fire as well as a means of resolving the problems of down-draught. The Georgian chimneys were constructed, for aesthetic reasons, lower than those of previous periods and so the pots also helped increase their height, whilst reducing the bulk of the stack. But even then, as Alec Clifton-Taylor has pointed out in *The Pattern of English Building* (1971), "... good craftsmen took care to sink them within the flues so that they did not project more than about two inches, and were therefore invisible from directly below. This excellent practice is still sometimes followed today, but much less often than it might be, for it is fully consonant with both the essentials of good chimeny construction, which are to reduce the size of the aperture at the top of the flue, and to contrive that the wind shall not blow across a horizontal plane but impinge against an edge."

The open fire was completely inadequate for industrial and commercial use. For such use the most efficient method was the closed stove, an improved form of which was developed in the late 18th century by William Strut. This latter development consisted of the passing of air over a heating surface. The system was installed in numerous cotton mills. The Belper Stove, invented in 1806, was a considerable advance on this idea. But the closed stove was soon replaced in many factories by a system of steam heating.

Steam heating was first installed by James Watt to heat his workshop in 1784. And in 1791 a patent for steam pipe heating was taken out by Mr Hoyle, a Yorkshireman from Halifax. An alternative system was the use of hot water pipes. The heating of greenhouses by such a system had first appeared in the early 18th century in Europe. The system was introduced into England in 1816.

The Landscape Garden 1714 - 1830

The early Georgian garden really heralds the English passion for gardening as we know it today. Up until this period, gardens were very formal, surrounding the house, and used more as outdoor salons. The plants were grouped, planted and clipped to resemble large living tapestries, and furnished with topiary. Beyond this, the land was left as farm, field or hunting forest.

An early garden at Studley Royal, Yorkshire, begun around 1715 by John Aislabie, a chancellor of the Exchequor, was a definite departure from the earlier style. It is interesting because, although still incorporating asymmetrical formality, it is completely separate from the house.

Alexander Pope and Joseph Addison also began to advocate the delight of free form and the break away to allow trees and shrubs to develop their natural forms.

Pope totally ridiculed topiary, whilst Addison believed that nothing could touch Nature's own art and that man could simply enhance it as in a landscape painting. Stephen Switzer was one of the very few people to follow Addison's ideas and devised, in 1718, a much less formal estate plan, a forerunner of the "ferme ornee" which materialised some 20 years later when Philip Southcote continued the theme in forming a perimeter winding walk around his estate, bounded by beech trees, primroses, jonquils and snowdrops.

One of the designers to develop these ideas was William Kent, the architect who studied in Rome, under Benedetto Luti and became the factotum of the Earl of Burlington. He designed his gardens to contrast by their natural settings with the formality of his architecture.

He created his early gardens at Rousham Hall, Oxfordshire (1734–41) and Chiswick House, where, with Lord Burlington, he formed a garden with a meandering stream and winding path through shrubs and trees. Stowe, Buckinghamshire, which was originally an enclosed geometrical garden, was embarked upon by Kent around 1730 softening Bridgeman's more formal endeavours and transforming the gardens into a lyrical landscape with open vistas and woodland glades. The small classical temples were viewed across tranquil water, in the shape of two irregularly-formed lakes, created from one large expanse of water.

Kent also designed the gardens of Alexander Pope's villa at Twickenham, Middlesex at about the same time as Stowe and a few years later, Richmond Gardens, Surrey, where be built a Merlin's Cave. Horace Walpole wrote that Kent's principle was, "that nature abhors a straight line".

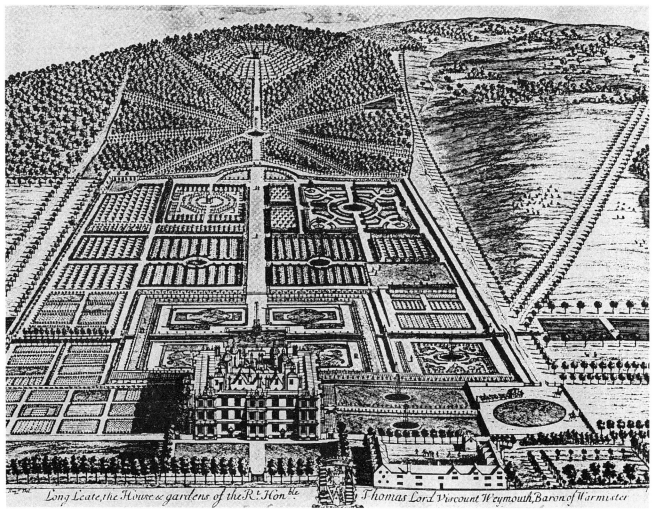

Long Leate, the House & gardens of the Rt. Honble ... Thomas Lord Viscount Weymouth, Baron of Warmister

Drawing by Kip and Knyff, c.1700, of the gardens designed by George London for Longleat.

After Kent's death in 1748, Joseph Spence continued along the same lines, becoming the champion of the minor gentry. He carried out practical designs with a keen eye for colour, plants and scents.

Around this period, the ha-ha came into being as a concealed division between garden and grounds, and this caused no visual interruption to the flowing landscape. It also acted as a sunken fence keeping stock out of the garden. The English nobility now began, in earnest, to plant trees in vast numbers creating new parks, crossed by bridleways and avenues. The underlying theme was to merge park and "improved" countryside. Up until this time, agriculture had followed the strip system with one man farming a few small fields bounded by natural division. This was changed by the Enclosure Acts which produced much larger fields yielding far more food per acre. It also changed the look of the countryside.

100

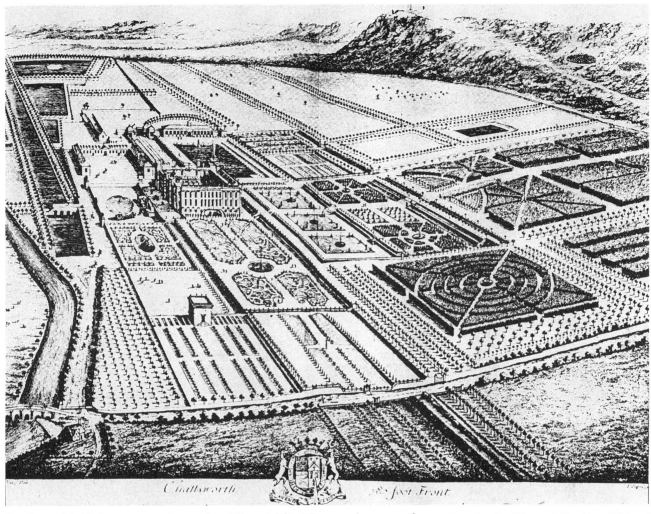

Chattsworth   foot Front

In the mid-18th century, Lancelot 'Capability' Brown became the darling of the Georgian 'glitterati'. As a young man, in charge of the kitchen garden at Stowe, he was required to show the nobility around and was able to project his ideas to the very people who were to become his clients. Known by his nickname for posterity, it was derived from his habit of saying, "There are great capabilities here". He loved sweeping curves topped with clumps of trees of a single species, mostly grand English natives, such as oak, beech, elm and limes. He loved the still waters of lakes and his first major achievement was the creation of one at Wakefield Lodge for the Duke of Grafton. From this success he moved on to Blenheim Palace where the splendour of the lake mirrored the architectural bridge of John Vanburgh. The harmonious patterns and noble sense of scale he brought to his landscapes swept away all the fussy, geometric designs of the 17th century and probably changed more of England's acreage than any man before or since.

Drawing by Kip and Knyff, c.1700, of the gardens at Chatsworth designed by George London.

101

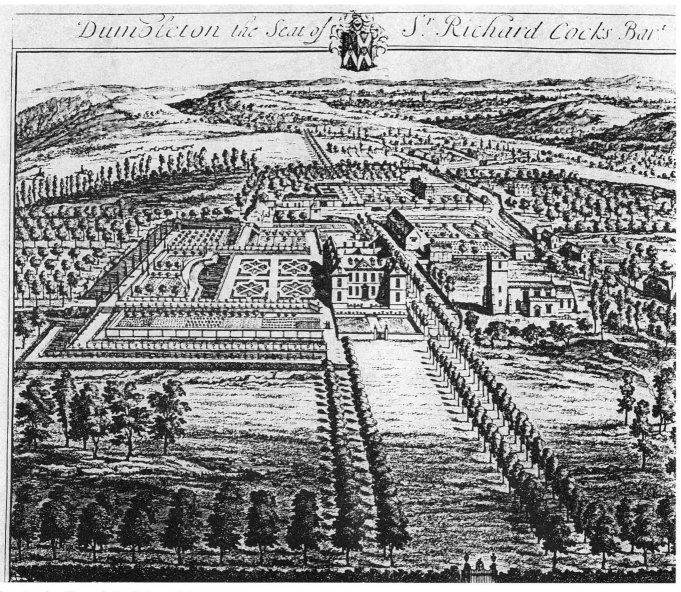

Drawing by Kip and Knyff from *Britannia Illustrata ..,* **pub. 1707, of Dumbleton, Gloucestershire.**

However, there were people who disagreed with this approach and preferred the more romantic, picturesque style led by Sir Uvedale Price and the artist, Rev William Gilpin, advocating well-placed rock formations and rotting tree trunks as being more in keeping than Brown's huge sweeping landscapes. Others created a still more poetic style using elements of surprise in their landscapes. Small grottoes, classical statues, gothic ruins were stumbled upon through the grounds. Chinoiserie details were also in evidence but the enthusiasm for this style waned in England by 1760, but became fashionable in Europe and known as the 'jardin anglais'.

Many new town squares had central landscaped gardens, as at The Circus, Bath. Late 18th century engraving.

Exotic flowers were grown, as increasingly world trade and travel had resulted in foreign plants being introduced. They were cultivated in glass houses and flower gardens near to the house, but, in general, flowers were not an intrinsic part of the overall vision of the landscape park.

It is interesting to note that the gentian was one of the first plants chosen for the gardens of Blenheim, because of its brilliant blue flowers.

Some of the new specimens brought from foreign lands were nurtured in the Royal Botanic Gardens, started in 1759 by Princess Augusta, mother of George III, on three hectares of London, her husband's property. The chinoiserie pagoda, a fifty metre tower, was designed by Sir William Chambers, as was the Orangery. The Palm House, designed by Decimus Burton, came later, in 1845. These gardens, now universally known simply as Kew, became the property of the nation in 1841.

The growing of fresh fruit and vegetables for the table was of great importance to the upper class Georgian household, to feed not just the family and large household staff, but to support the comparatively lavish scale of entertainment. Despite this the kitchen garden was often sited a distance from the house, even as far away as half a mile,

103

being dismissed as unsightly. One can only imagine the rows that must have developed between cook and gardener below stairs!

A gardener's life was certainly not an easy one; the average weekly pay was about 10 shillings, whilst a head gardener could expect about 40 pounds a year, compared to the butler's fifty, although they did enjoy free board and lodging. The highest wages a jobbing gardener could expect was about 3 shillings a day but was expected to provide his own tools. However, even this must have been preferable to the Russian gardeners who were obliged to sleep under a mat in the garden, their toes exposed to the night air as early-warning frost detectors;

The amount of work and skill that was put into produce was remarkable. Melons and cucumbers had been highly prized since their introduction in the 1570s and asparagus was forced outdoors from the early 1800s, although it had been available under glass since the 17th century. By the end of the Georgian period 30 varieties of melons were known. Peaches, apricots, nectarines, and even citrus fruit were grown under glass, often in the most elaborately constructed orangeries or conservatories built at great expense. That at Bretton Hall, Yorkshire, cost £14,000 to put up in 1829, mainly due to the high cost of glass. Tomatoes, however, were not a greenhouse plant. They were considered to be dangerous and were treated as half hardy annuals for a decorative effect in flower borders, if used at all.

We have lost a lot of the skills, patience and dedication of the Georgian gardener – the magnificent King Frederick striped tulip is now only history and the 400 varieties of pansy have sadly dwindled, but we gained the broad, sweeping vistas, and the sheer breadth of vision that so conjures up in the mind the very greenness of English gardens.

The Cottager and the Small Farmer

Whilst the 18th century was Britain's "golden age" with the affluent towns of the period resplendent with the handsome façades of Queen Anne and Georgian houses designed to accommodate the needs of a rising middle class, it was also an age of marked disparity between rich and poor. In England and Wales, the chief occupation was still largely agriculture, and in an attempt to improve the housing standards for the farm labourer, cottages were erected in the neighbouring villages by the more enlightened landowners. But such improvements in housing standards took time to reach the less populated areas. The sunken, one-roomed dwellings recorded in Somerset in the 1880s or the cottages of turf or dry-stone walling common in Northumberland and the West Riding in the 19th century, are no improvement on the Cornish husbandman's earth-walled, thatch-roofed house of the early 18th century. One major improvement from the Saxon hut to Stuart cottage was not in the size, but in having walls of a man's height which meant that the floor no longer had to be sunk below ground level.

Cottages of this sort were built later in two different ways. One way was to build better versions of the old houses, more spacious and of stouter materials. The second and more significant way was to build lofty open halls adapted from upper class houses. Lofts began to appear in the early 16th century and by the late 16th century, the two storey house was standard throughout the south-east. These houses usually had three rooms, but in Devon, Cornwall and Somerset, the one-roomed house was still being built and it was not until the late 19th century that the two-roomed house was developed in Western and Southern England.

By the 18th century the rural labourers still only lived in a one-roomed cottage, sometimes with a lean-to shed, or outshut. Generally, they were better off than their European counterparts. As a result of improvements in agriculture methods, better bread and more meat was produced. Whilst the rural migrants in the towns often starved, the farm labourer ate meat once or twice a week, supplied their own bacon and eggs and made their own bread from rye or bran. But the the 1740s rural life had begun to change rapidly. The wealthier landowners had already started enclosing their estates, evicting tenants and destroying their homes. This process, which created the hedgerows of the typical English countryside, was accelerated by the parliamentary Enclosure Acts of 1761–1845.

Evicted farmers began to establish themselves on the less fertile moors, hills and mountains, while the landless labourer began

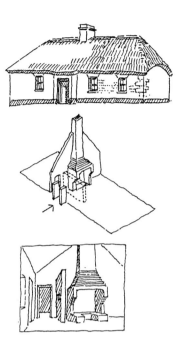

Early 19th century farmhouse, Co. Fermanagh. Now in the Ulster Folk Museum, it is a characteristic farmhouse of South Ulster complete with hipped roof and brick chimney with the hearth screened from the entrance by the jamb wall. In the jamb wall is a little spy-window.

Labourer's dwelling, Duncrun townland, Co. Derry. Now in the Ulster Folk Museum, it was built in the mid 18th century, and is characteristic of the north - west with bed outshut and thatch roof fastened by ropes.

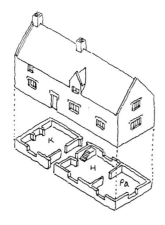

So strong was the vernacular tradition of the 17th century cob built houses, such as this Yeoman's house at Nettacott, Upton Pyne, Devon, that this *timeless way* of building lasted well into the 18th century. Diagram based on M.W. Barley's work published in *The English Farmhouse and Cottage*.

weaving, spinning, basket-making and other home crafts to earn a little extra.

Bad harvests in the 1760s and 1770s and the wars with France, forced prices up, but wages were not increased. Under the Act of Settlement of 1662, anyone was eligible for some kind of relief from the parish where he was born or had settled. But many landowners, in order to reduce their liability for poor rate, let cottages decay and, in some cases pulled them down. By doing this they could also force so-called undesirables to move.

In the late 18th century some liberals, appalled by conditions for many cottagers, began to raise questions. An agriculturalist and land valuer named Nathaniel Kent pointed out in his book, *Hints to Gentlemen of Landed Property* (1775), the absurdity of landlords providing elaborate stables and kennels while neglecting the cottages, for it was the cottagers who would provide the hands to cultivate the land. Kent's book was the first to contain plans for model cottages. John Wood, the designer of the Royal Crescent, Bath, produced an architectural book in 1781 devoted entirely to cottages insisting, among other things, on regularity, which to him constituted beauty. By the late 18th century some landlords saw cottage building simply as an artistic exercise. After 1780, designs for cottages began to appear in architectural pattern books. The emphasis moved away from Wood's more classical stance to a celebration of the purely rustic and picturesque.

James Malton in his *Essays on British Cottage Architecture* (1798), suggested an irregularity in colour, texture and materials sufficient to produce an effect of a painting. In *Sketches in Architecture* (1798), Sir John Soane included designs for cottages combining rusticity with the regularity of antiquity. The designs for a number of model villages were much influenced by his sketches, but it was a minority who built the picturesque; most built the purely utilitarian.

The vast increase in cotton from the cotton mills in the 1770s led to the amazing expansion of weaving throughout south-east Lancashire. It was the loom and not the cotton mill which attracted immigrants in their thousands and small farmers and agricultural labourers entered the trade and became weavers. The old loom shops could not cope, so new weavers' cottages with loom shops rose up in every direction. The golden age of the trade was between 1788 and 1803.

Between 1790 and 1810 it was a matter of policy to increase the dependence of reserves of cheap labour for the convenience of the farmer at haymaking and harvest as well as for roadmaking and fencing. Some gentry, particularly in the north, saw the French wars as a means of reducing wages, with higher prices and fewer jobs. Over-population of the commons by cottagers and squatters antagonised the small proprietor, while panic and class struggle, inflamed in the aristocracy by the French Revolution, led to greater exploitation by master or servant. The wars curtailed the activities of the urban reformers and more caring gentry. A new argument was added to the arguments of greed, that of social discipline, and the commons were now seen as dangerous centres of indiscipline.

Parliamentary Enclosures

Land fell into fewer hands after the dissolution of the monasteries in the 1530s, which resulted in teh subsequent development of the large Tudor estates and the Great Rebuilding. This was followed by the turmoil of the Civil War and then the age of parliamentary enclosure and Georgian prosperity.

Piecemeal enclosure had been carried out since the 15th century, but the landscape of England had not changed noticeably until the mid-18th century when the Georgian planners created the *modern* countryside, that is the countryside we know today, a countryside of scattered farms and fields bordered by hedgerows. The great advantage of enclosure was that the more successful farmer, now independent of his neighbour, was free to introduce radical changes in the growing of crops and breeding of cattle. Whilst these enclosures made agriculture more efficient, it also meant that much of the land fell into the hands of a few, wealthy men who let it to tenant farmers. Enclosure required a considerable capital expenditure. Whilst the rewards for the wealthy were enormous, the agricultural labourer, who, with his small allotment and his common rights, had eked out a precarious living, now lost even that. The small, peasant farmer suffered equally. Lacking the necessary capital for enclosure, he too joined the swelling ranks of the rural poor along with the smaller tenant farmer, evicted from his land for being unprofitable. But the more intelligent and industrious yeomen farmers found ready work managing the new, large farms created by the landlords' enclosures.

There were few Enclosure Acts in the early 18th century, but by the mid-18th century the momentum had increased as wealthy landowners began to realise the considerable value, agriculturally, of such enclosures. By the 1740s there were 38 such Acts, rising to 156 in the 1750s; 424 in the 1760s; 642 in the 1770s; 906 in the 1800s.

The enclosures and subsequent merging of the farms, meant that many village street farms became redundant. They were converted into the maximum number of cottages together with their barns and cowhouses. The converted cottages were then rented. But the 18th century farmer realised that he could not keep his labour force without building cottages for them and soon the tied cottage was developed for the married labourer. The single man lived in his employer's house; from the Elizabethan period onwards the yeoman's houses had

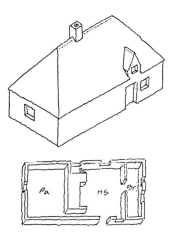

In the early 18th century, the unmarried labourer was often housed in the parlour or garret of his employer. The married labourer would often build his own cottage in the open village. Such a cottage would generally be built of mud and stud in the tradition passed on from the 17th century. In Lincolnshire, the tradition since the 17th century was for the studs to be covered externally by mud rendering, whilst internally they would be exposed.

(a)

(b)

(c)

18th century Wales was bequeathed many well-built, compactly-planned, two-celled houses of the 16th and 17th century. Typical examples are these sturdy, stone built houses at Ffestiniog, (a) and Maentwrog (b) both in Merioneth. By the 18th century many such buildings would be embedded in a range of farm buildings. Another example is this Yeoman's house at Tregynon, Powys (c).

chambers or parlours for servants. Nearly every farmhouse in the East Midlands used garrets for bedrooms.

Between 1760 and 1867 over seven million acres of common land was enclosed on the grounds that it would provide for more efficient farming. The cottager was deprived of his grazing rights and his four acres of land around the cottage was reduced to a little over half an acre. Compensation was provided in the form of allotments, but this provision was generally totally inadequate.

The Farm Labourers' Cottages

According to M. W. Barley in *The English Farmhouse and Cottage,* it was rare, before 1700, to build cottages to let. It was only the married farmworker who needed a cottage. This he would build himself on the wastelands of the open village. As in the late 17th century, the unmarried labourer continued to be housed in the parlour or garret of his employer. In some instances, the mansarded roofs of some farmhouses were modified with dormers to provide some comfortable accommodation. Many were only one-and-a-half storeys high, with dormer windows in the thatched roof. They were usually one room wide but there was often a second, smaller service room, sometimes added in an outshut later.

Long rows of houses were built similar to the purpose-built housing of the 19th century industrial worker. Rows of semi-detached cottages were also erected. But much of this building was in Southern England, for the northern farmer was more concerned with providing lodging above a barn or byre for unmarried labourers than with building cottages. The cottages that were built were usually smaller than those

The model village of Milton Abbas, the repetitive white walled, thatch-roofed cottages designed by Chambers.

Model cottages designed by George Dance in 1806 at East Stratton, Hampshire. Marvellous group of thatch-roofed, brick-built semi-detached cottages, entry to each via a projecting porch in the outshuts along the gable ends. Of particular interest are the timber casements, the windows designed to slide horizontally.

in the south. Houses were one storey in height, often with only one room. On some of the large 19th century Northumberland farms, these one-storeyed, one bedroomed houses were built in rows.

Radical developments in housing for the labourer were left to the more enlightened landlords. The 18th century was the golden age of landscape design when landlords fashioned their estates along Virgilian lines. The agricultural economy of East Anglia at this time was particularly prosperous, and one landlord, Lord Orford, discovered that his new park and lake at Chippenham, in Cambridgeshire, had swallowed up half the village, so he built a new one in 1712, on lines more suited to his own taste. Norfolk was particularly renowned for the quality of its farm cottages; crusading agricultural reformers, like Coke of Holkham, rich from their profitable new farming methods, could afford to build good-quality cottages.

Towards the late 18th and early 19th century, the major distinction was between the open village, where land could be bought or rented for building, and those which were closed and belonged to one owner who would control its development. Following the enclosures, many cottages had been demolished and towards the end of the 18th century cottagers were increasingly housed in 'model' villages. One of the best known is Nuneham Courtney, in Oxfordshire. The epitomy of Georgian patronage, the old village and church was demolished in the 1760s to be replaced by a classical landscape complete with model village of chequer brick tenants' cottages, forge, inn, curate's house and church as an ornamental temple in the park under the auspices of the first Earl of Harcourt. Another example of 'embarking' was that of Milton Abbas, Dorset. Here families evicted from the original village, demolished because it interrupted the view from the landlord's house, were rehoused in 1775, in two-storey high, whitewashed and thatched roofed cottages, spread out on a continuous stretch of lawn flanking a single, winding street.

Farmhouses

The agrarian revolution of the 18th century was a prolific period for farmbuilding, especially in the lowlands of England. Farmhouses and cottages were grouped within the village under the old system of strip farming. The village farmhouse, as such, was generally of the long-house type. As the enclosures acts took effect a pattern of larger, more compact farmsteads was created with new, more fashionable-looking farmhouses being built in spacious complexes, some distance away from the village. The older village farmhouses, now redundant, were generally subdivided into a series of farmworkers' cottages.

The Georgian farmhouse was not unlike its town equivalent. By the 1730s the smaller farmhouses had a symmetrical, classically designed facade of three bays with a central entrance, flanked by windows. The ground floor accommodation consisted of a hall and parlour with a staircase, planned opposite the central entrance, dividing the two rooms. Both hall and parlour would have a fireplace on the gable wall. Earlier 18th century farmhouses had had detached kitchens. Gradually the kitchen became an integral part of the house. With the more profitable agricultural methods, larger farmhouses were needed with increased storage space. Typical of these larger farmhouses was a five

Farmhouse, Crossguns, Co. Meath. 18th century houses such as this, often occupied by struggling minor gentry, generally had a parlour and kitchen with lodging rooms above.

House at Crolly, Co. Donegal.

House with bedroom over byre, Crolly, Co. Donegal.

Typical farm cottage with range of farm buildings added later, in Llandegfan, Anglesey.

Cob-walled farmhouse at Woodbury, Devon, built c.1700.

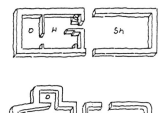

The traditional longhouse was still to be found on the edges of Dartmoor from the late 16th until the early 18th century. The simplest form of longhouse (a) consists of a single storey entry and through passage open to the shippon and used by both man and beast. Increasingly there was a need to separate the shippon from the through passage. In the late 16th century a wood partition was common (b). By the mid 17th century the wood partition was replaced by a substantial stone wall.

bay house, two storeys in height with a central entrance plus an attic storey. The attic storey, usually low and ill-ventilated, was intended originally for storage, but the need to house unmarried farmworkers, as well as servants, was such that many were lodged in these garrets as well. With the advent of the larger farmhouse, many of the small farmhouses were let as cottages for the farm workers. Little provision was made for rental accommodation before 1700. But with the growing labour needs of large scale arable farming, the more enlightened landlords began to build terraced cottages for the rural labourers. The importance of well built, well planned farm buildings in contributing to a healthy agricultural economy was underlined by the Board of Agriculture, created in 1793, when it published its unique county by county survey.

Laithe house built at Eccleshill, West Yorkshire, in 1754.

Characteristic farmhouse built at Trefdraeth, Anglesey in 1731. Note the outshut to the rear.

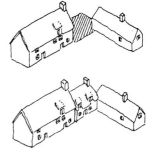

18th century cottage built between an earlier terrace and barn at Exton, Leicestershire.

Many of the century's great architects turned their attention to the design of farm buildings, as an ancillary to the great houses for which they were responsible, as John Weller points out in *The History of the Farmstead*. Samuel Wyatt designed the Great Barn at Holkham Hall for Thomas William Coke in 1790 and John Soane designed a cow-barn for Burn Hall, Co Durham, in 1784. Numerous others, including Robert Adam and Henry Holland, designed model estates. I. Leatham, writing in *The General View of the Agriculture of the East Riding of Yorkshire* (1774), suggested that in the ideal farmstead, " . . . farm offices, when properly built, should form a square; and all offices should be placed as conveniently and as near each other as possible; the fold yard should be in the centre; and the pump and watering trough should be near the back door where the cattle should be watered, to prevent the loss of their dung . . . the stackyard should adjoin the barn, to prevent waste by carrying the corn from a distance; and the granary should, if possible, be over the carriage-shed, or any other place where it can be built in a situation equally cool and airy, and not over a stable." Most writers of the period addressed the domestic aspects of farm life. In *Rural Architecture* (1802), John Plaw concentrated on the design of farmhouses and cottages as did James Malton when he published his *An Essay on Rural Architecture* in 1803.

Greenhouse, Tullowmagimma, Co. Carlow. Solid, box-like farmhouse of the late 18th century with pedimented central section with dressed stone surrounds to the door and an attractive fanlight above.

113

Mid 18th century farmhouse at Easter Happrew, Peebleshire.

Below: The Great Barn, Holkham Hall, Norfolk, c.1790. Apart from isolated attempts to produce decent housing for farm workers, the agricultural revolution meant new, more spacious farm buildings such as this remarkable structure.

Below right: Many new farms were built in the late 18th and early 19th century. This brick built arcaded cart shed is at Swallow Grange, Lincolnshire. The cart shed was open, whilst above it was a granary store.

However, in James Gandy's *The Rural Architect* published in 1805, there is an illustration for a Royal Institute of Agricultural Education along with his description of dwelling types.

114

The Parsonage

The church and manor house were the major architectural set pieces of the village. The church pre-eminent in size and position, had played a real and active role in medieval village life. The manor house, invariably a stately Georgian structure in stone or brick, was the centre of village government. The church and manor house provided the necessary nucleus around which the village grew. The major fabric of the village consisted of small cottages and terraces, but in the middle of the social rung were a series of not insubstantial houses built for the bailiffs and stewards. On a par with these was the Parsonage – architecturally often less sophisticated, particularly those built in the late 17th century when parsons were first allowed to marry. Many of these houses had thatch roofs and earth or brick floors downstairs. The one exception was the parlour which invariably had a boarded floor as did the chambers upstairs. In Lincolnshire and Nottinghamshire in the late 17th and early 18th centuries, some floors upstairs were often of gypsum plaster or lime. As M. W. Barley points out, in the early 18th century " . . . walls were white-washed, for wall painting and painted cloths had gone out of fashion, and farmers and parsons could not afford the flock wall-papers which were now beginning to be made." In the more substantial of the parsonage houses, a necessary house was included amongst the outbuildings.

The Vicarage, Penshurst, Kent.
This is the classic view of the vicarage and church, the early 18th century brick front of the vicarage peeping over the mellow brick wall encircling the churchyard. The house behind the brick facade is older.

115

Many pattern books of the mid-18th century suggested that something fairly straigntforward and utilitarian was the most appropriate building for a parsonage. In *The Complete Body of Architecture,* published in 1756, Isaac Ware suggested that the typical parsonage may have " ... upon the level ground, if it be dry and wholesome ... an entrance from the principal door; and each side a parlour. In front may be the stair-case; and over these the lodging rooms. Behind may be placed a kitchen and wash house which need be no more than sheds well covered; and, as most who devote themselves to a country life take the amusements of reading and riding, beyond the right hand parlour may be a study, covered as the kitchen, and beyond to the left a stable."

Parsons supplemented their income by farming their *glebe* lands. The glebe land, on which the parsonage was built, was land belonging to or yielding revenue to a parish church or ecclesiastical benefice. The Enclosure movement, which greatly improved farm profits, also created more profitable glebe farms.

The big landowners had livings to bestow as did some university colleges. The former, in order to strengthen their standing in a locality, would often buy up the rights to present an incumbant of their own choice. Many parsonages were rebuilt or greatly improved by such patrons. And many parsons saw such an endowed living as being something on a par with a fellowship at a college; many endowments were accepted more as a privilege and hand in hand with such an honour was the opportunity to live in a house of a quality superior to many of the smaller farmhouses around.

Some parsons were well off in their own right and were quite happy to construct their own houses which were invariably bequeathed to the living. They preferred rather *modern* houses, Palladian if possible, often sited in more prominent positions some distance from the churchyard. But the large sums spent on such houses was disapproved of by some. William Cowper (1731–1800), the author son of the rector of Great Berkhampstead, was a champion of the oppressed and in his long epic poem, *The Task* (1785), wrote of his disapproval of such improvements, pointing out that " ... it is no uncommon thing to see the parsonage house ... in exceeding good repair, while the Church perhaps has scarce any other roof than the ivy that grows over it." Whilst some held more than one living and lived in quite salubrious surroundings, by the late 18th century the majority of the clergy were quite poor, many living still in rudimentary cottages with earth floors.

116

The Smaller House and Cottages of the Countryside

This was the golden age of English house building of a quality of craftsmanship and design the like of which had not been seen before. The handsome rectangular or square blocks with elegant porch and graceful front door and largely symmetrical facade, were seen as suitable abodes by the rising middle class. It has been estimated that there are, surviving today, over one million small Georgian houses built between the years 1700 and 1830. There are the grander winged mansions of the aristocracy and well-to-do, but it is those smaller Georgian houses, found in the more affluent towns and villages of the South-East, Midlands and the North which are of particular interest, for it is in these that we find an architecture unaffected by the regional characteristics of the vernacular tradition. The pattern followed, as such, was that of a restrained Dutch Palladianism of stone dressed brick, first imported to England following the Restoration in 1660 and subsequently assimilated, and by the 18th century, an English national character was established.

A small Georgian house in Kent or Sussex was little different in plan from those found in the towns and villages of Lincolnshire and the North Midlands. The principal difference was in the materials used, which were invariably local, and the fact that those houses in the South-East would have been built some fifty to a hundred years earlier than those found in the Midlands and North. But although there was a

Late 18th century town house with a front parlour shop.

18th century house at Odiham, Hampshire.

A street of 18th century terraces, Bridport, Dorset.

117

Adam style entrance porch with segmental pediment, The High Street, Lewes, Sussex.

Georgian doorway at Chichester.

Three storey terrace at Bradford-on-Avon.

great expansion in house building, many of the so-called Georgian houses were, in fact, Tudor buildings re-faced in the more fashionable style of the Georgians. Such were the social pressures, that few amongst the rising middle class could afford not to live in a house designed in the modern, Georgian style. However, there were economic ways of transforming the fronts of existing buildings with a complete new symmetrical facade with high parapets so that the only timber stud work visible was down the sides or rear of such houses. Casement windows were replaced by sash windows; stone effects were created by scoring plaster or stucco; plaster was used to simulate stone dressings to brickwork; timber boards were tongued and grooved and then scored with vertical joints in semblance of stone blocks and mathematical tiles were used to give a brick-like appearance while

Handsome Georgian town houses, Bridport, Dorset.

The pedimented entrance of a Georgian terrace house, The High Street, Lewes, Sussex.

Particularly fine entrance porch, Lewes House, The High Street, Lewes, Sussex.

avoiding the brick taxes. The best examples are to be found in the Sussex town of Lewes.

While the alterations to the medieval houses of Tenterden in Kent, were made by numerous craftsmen, Burford, in Oxfordshire, had many of its High Street Tudor built houses re-fronted by no lesser a figure than the redoubtable Christopher Kempster, who was Sir Christopher Wren's friend, and a mason employed on the building of St Paul's. When work was completed on the Cathedral in 1708,

119

Terrace housing, Bradford-on-Avon.

Georgian porch, Chichester, Sussex.

Kempster returned to Burford, near to which he owned a quarry. There must have been a whole army of unemployed masons looking for work when he began to re-front many of the old houses in the classical style adapted by Wren for domestic buildings. Thus you have the carefully prepared faces of ashlar work, no ornaments, high sash windows, broad, shallow, mouldings, and simplicity of outline. Yet go down the little alleys to the rear, and there you have the Tudor structures untouched. Whilst these handsome Georgian houses, built on a large scale, transcended the vernacular tradition, many more houses were built which were entirely vernacular.

120

The West Country

Whilst houses built of unhewn granite, found lying on the ground around, are characteristic of Devon and Cornwall, Cob Construction, until quite recently, was the preferred material. Typical of cottage construction from the Middle Ages onwards, cob, a mix of clay and straw, was thrown on to the wall and then trodden down and left to dry in the sun. The walling was slowly built up in layers over several months. Windows, door frames and floor joists were built into the walling at the same time. There was no supporting timber frame to the wall. The cob walls were often built on a low stone foundation over which they projected an inch or so as protection against vermin and damp. The corners of the houses were generally rounded off to avoid cracking, the most common weakness of cob walling. Walls were whitewashed or colourwashed, and the normal roofing material was a cover of thatch.

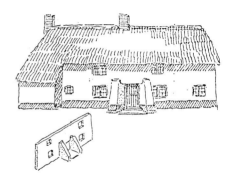

Cob cottage, Branscombe, Seaton, Devonshire. The walls, built up in layers up to 12 inches high, were generally between 2 and 4 ft in thickness. In this example, the wall around the entrance has been buttressed.

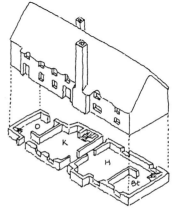

Diagram based on Maurice Barley's study of the characteristic house of the Ham Hill area of Somerset from the 16th until the early 18th century. The kitchen was separated from the Hall by a cross passage. Partitioned off to one end of the Hall was a parlour. The principal bedroom has a dormer.

Cottage orné, Budleigh Salterton, Devonshire. Complete with thatched widow's walk, it was built by a local ship owner in the early 19th century.

Cob cottages, Outer Cove, Devonshire.

121

Cob cottages, Inner Cove, Devon.

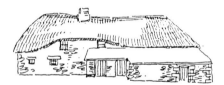

Longhouse, Widecombe-in-the-Moor, Devonshire. By the late 17th and early 18th century most longhouses had separate entrances to the through passage and shippon.

Cottage, Blaise Hamlet, Avon. Designed by John Nash (1810-12), it was the first completely *informal* model village designed in the novel Picturesque manner beloved by the late 18th century writers and painters, such as Uvedale Price, James Molton and David Laing.

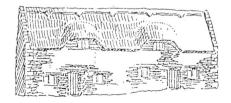

Whilst many farm labourers were provided with minimal shelter, the comfort, health, safety and security of horses, as Dr R.W. Brunskill has pointed out, was crucial. In the less dry counties, spacious, well lit airy stables were typical of the late 18th and early 19th centuries. This example, at Stoke-sub-Hamdon, Somerset, has two stables set side by side, under the thatched roof. The eyebrow dormers give access to the hay loft above the stables.

The longhouse tradition, involved family quarters at one end with cattle installed at the other, lower end, so that the slurry could be drained down the hill, and all under the same roof. In the 13th century, when it first developed, the two parts were open to the other. By the 16th century a partition and access separated the two, the cross passage providing access not to the house, but to the shippon. By the mid-17th century a stone wall replaced the wooden partition and a separate entrance was opened into the shippon. A door leading off the cross passage connected the main house to the shippon. By the early 18th century the separation between shippon and the main house became more distinct. The house itself was greatly enlarged.

Cob cottages, Inner Cove, Devon.

Brown's Farmhouse, Woodbury, Devon. Built of cob in 1700, it is a four bay house with a lobby entrance axially aligned with the chimney stack. The roof space over the end bay to the left, was used for storage and has a loft door in the gable end.

Houses at Dinder, Somerset, showing the characteristic gabled dormers. One of several attractive terraces and cottages built in the grounds of Dinder House, a handsome Georgian manor house.

Many of the smaller buildings of this period in the mountain and moorland districts, such as Dartmoor, the Isle of Man, North Wales and Scottish Highlands, were built of unquarried stone. In Cornwall, for example, blocks of granite were used producing a simple but solid building. The walls were usually two feet or more in thickness. Often the stones were bedded in earth and then plastered or whitewashed over. Gaps between the boulders were filled with small stones or rubble. Few builders were able to construct roofs to span more than

St Mary's Buildings, Wells Road, Bath. Modest terrace of artisans' houses stepping neatly down a steep slope, the whole composition held together by the sweeping curve of the crowning cornice. Early 19th century.

123

Beaufort Square, Bath, designed by John Straham between 1727-36.

Square and green surrounded by unassuming cottage made memorable by fine proportion and detail. Straham was the great rival of John Wood. The south side of the square is occupied by the principal front of the Theatre Royal, designed by George Dance c. 1804.

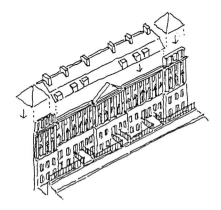

Axonometric of north side of Queen Square, Bath. Designed and built by John Wood the Elder between 1728-36.

one room across and so plans were enlarged by adding on additional bays, by an outshut or by a right-angled projection.

Cottages built of a local quarried stone had thinner walls, between eighteen inches to two feet thick, the internal cavity being filled with rubble or small stones.

The Southern Counties

The form and character of vernacular building, in contrast to the so-called *polite* architecture, was not constrained by the vagaries of taste, but by the limits of the programme, availability of materials, cost and technical expertise. From one century to the next you find the tried and tested craftsmanship of the local builder perpetuated in one building after another. The most characterful of the vernacular buildings in this region are the cob walled cottages. Whilst many small houses and cottages were constructed in timber along the borders of Berkshire, Wiltshire and Hampshire, it was rare to find timber building towards the west, in Dorset, where cob walling, and

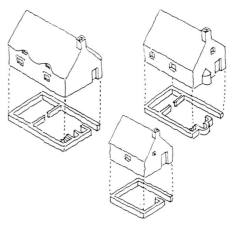

As M. W. Barley has pointed out in *The English Farmhouse and Cottage,* the small house, typical in the southern part of the limestone belt of the Cotswolds in the late 17th century, was characterised by an entrance in the gable end. By the early 18th century the entrance was generally positioned in the main frontage. The smallest plan probably had a ladder to the loft.

Church Cottage, Swindon, Wiltshire. Timber frame, thatched-roof cottage built 1700 and consisting of two ground storey rooms with attic storey above.

The Lions, Bridgwater, Somerset. Built c.1730.

125

Westbury House, Bradford-on-Avon. Handsome early Georgian town house standing on the south bank of the river.

Cottage built of Wiltshire limestone, at Stockton. This type of cottage, walled with random rubble and often roofed with thatch, is found in the counties traversed or crossed by the limestone belt, such as Dorset, North-West Wiltshire, Somerset, Gloucestershire, Oxfordshire, Leicestershire, Northamptonshire and Lincolnshire; throughout the 17th and 18th century.

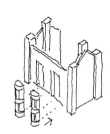

Hope House, Woodstock, c.1720, sits amongst unpretentious Georgian houses. The bow windows were added c.1780. Designed by one of the craftsmen-designers of the lesser country houses, the influence of Blenheim is especially strong in the boldly articulated gable end with its three tiers of blind windows, the two upper tiers crowned by huge keystones.

One of numerous park buildings and follies built in the grounds of Badminton House, Great Badminton, Gloucestershire, probably by Thomas Wright, c.1750, who built the Root House and Ragged Castle. The square planned lodge has four round corner towers and a central chimney crowning the pyramidal roof. A second chimney was added later.

126

occasionally stone, with a thatch roof was more common. The cob cottages of Dorset were built with chalk mixed with clay, and straw was used to bind the mixture together, but in the sandy districts heather was used instead. The walling was then built up in layers of two to three feet high and two feet in thickness, each layer being left to settle for a day or two before another was added. But cob walling was laborious and the structural limitations it imposed restricted its use almost entirely to buildings of a humbler status, like the small farmhouse and cottage. The typical plan of such houses in the late 17th and throughout the 18th century, was of one or two rooms. Few cottages had storage space, larders or sculleries. The bake-oven was generally built into the wall beside the fireplace. Originally a brick or plaster hood was cantilevered out in the room over the hearth. This was rather unstable and gradually it was replaced by bringing the whole chimney breast forward. Occasionally stone seats were hollowed out of the walls on either side of the fireplace. The early cottage staircase was a steep ladder, but this was replaced by a compact staircase built around a central newel or pillar and it was

Small Georgian terraces, Bridport, Dorset.

Spa Cottages, Lower Swell, Gloucestershire. Thought to have been designed by S P Cockerell, the architect of nearby Sezincote. The central block with decorative parapet, has Hindu-style motifs crowning the central porch and framing the flanking windows. A Chalybeate Spring was found her in 1807. One of the adjoining cottages was used originally as a Spa.

usually positioned in a corner by the chimney. Many floors were plastered by packing clay on wattle and laid between the joists, while red bricks, tiles or stone flags were used for the ground floors.

Many houses were built in Oxfordshire and Gloucestershire during the 17th century boom period as a result of the prosperous cloth industry. The warm, mellow limestone was quarried not only for the great house, but also the simple cottage. And it was the design of the latter that lingered on well into the 18th century, consolidating the form and character of Cotswold towns and villages. The dormer window, a product of the Middle Ages for making headroom in the roofspace, was transformed into one of the most distinctive features of

Early 19th century cottage orné. Originally a toll house on the main road leading out of Lyme Regis, Dorset. It has an octagonal plan, central chimney and delightful umbrella-like thatched roof.

Four bay brick built Georgian house, Blandford Forum, Dorset.

127

18th century street, Chichester, Sussex.

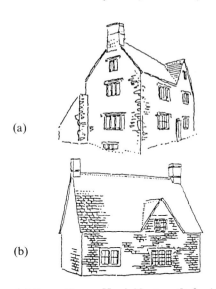

(a)

(b)

(a) Farm House, Hook Norton, Oxfordshire, c.1646. (b) Typical Cotswold cottage, Little Barrington, Gloucestershire. Such decent, straight-forward building was characteristic of the vernacular tradition in the region from the mid 17th to the 18th century.

the Cotswolds with the gabled dormer flush with the facades of the house. A third room called the backhouse or netherhouse was added to the hall and parlour of the farmhouse, often in an outshut under a lean-to roof. It was a general service room which gradually began to take on the function of kitchen or milkhouse. Chimneys were built either at the gabled end or in the centre of the house, and the use of stone made them both massive and simple, and limited the stacks to reactangular or square plans. Another distinctive feature, occasionally to be found in cottages aligning a village street, was an angular, bay window, often incorporating the front door and both built under the same stone-slated roof.

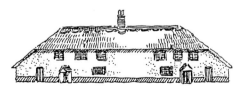

Cob cottage, Stinsford, Dorset.

Typical pair of early 19th century cottages, built in Upper Woodford, Wiltshire. Characteristic of this area is the chequerboard pattern of flint and stone.

Two storey terraces, Bridport, Dorset.

128

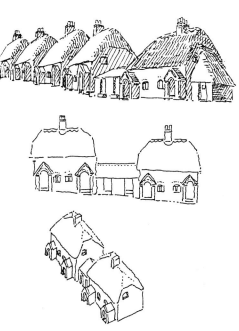

Five pairs of thatch-roofed, brick-built cottages c.1800. The bedrooms in the attic storey are lit by windows in the gable under the half-hipped roofs. The cottages are linked by single storey outbuildings.

In some areas stone was combined with flint in decorative banding. This was a common feature of houses built on the chalk uplands of Dorset from the mid-17th century onwards. Cottages built of rough stone, the stone usually found at random on the surrounding ground, are typical of Wiltshire parts of Hampshire, Dorset and Berkshire. Called pudding stone, this rough stone provided a fairly unpretentious looking material for building. Along the Dorset border with Wiltshire, some walls are built of a combination of pudding stone, brick and flint. The walls are nearly always whitewashed.

The countryside in the traditional agricultural areas was changing rapidly. By the beginning of the 18th century much of the land had

18th century brick houses, modest in scale and manner, stepping down a wide, but short village street, Hambledon, Hampshire. Some houses have porches or simple hoods over their entrances. The occasional house is whitewashed. The epitome of small-scale urbanisation.

129

Former 'keepers cottage', Yellowhand Wood, Dorset. This was the cottage described in Thomas Hardy's *Under the Greenwood Tree*. Yellowhand Wood, renamed Yalbury Wood for Hardy's Wessex tale, lies between Dorchester and Puddletown. Early 19th century.

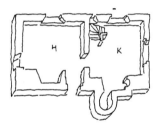

Two-cell Cotswold cottage, characteristic of the 17th and 18th century. The bake-oven was usually incorporated as shown, opening out of the fireplace in the kitchen.

Milton Abbas, Dorset. The village, built as a product of emparking c.1780, consists of pairs of whitewashed, thatch-roofed cottages set behind a broad grass verge along a winding road climbing a thickly wooded ridge of land. Half way up, on the right, stands a church designed by James Wyatt in 1786.

become heavily enclosed and the cottagers had become landless labourers. Life steadily became worse for the cottager. By the late 18th century, the first of the pioneering model villages were built here – Nuneham Courtney in Oxfordshire and Milton Abbas in Dorset. In the 1760s Nuneham Courtney, which consists of nineteen pairs of red-brick cottages, one-and-a-half storeys high, with dormers in the roof, was a replacement for the older village, demolished by Lord Harcourt, to make way for a classical landscape. It has been suggested that the older village was 'Sweet Auburn', the *Deserted Village* of Oliver Goldsmith's best known poem, published in 1770. The village, neatly aligning the Oxford Road, is a fine example of Georgian ribbon development. Milton Abbas is another, built as a replacement for the large village that had grown up around the old abbey. The remains of the abbey were incorporated into a new mansion built for the MP,

Two storey, three bay house, Blandford Forum, Dorset.

Entrance porch, Chichester, Sussex.

Entrance porch, Chichester, Sussex.

Joseph Damer, later the Earl of Dorchester. But the existing village was thought too much an eyesore, and a replacement, built in a wooded pass between the downs, was begun in 1773 with Capability Brown as landscape architect and Sir William Chambers, the architect of Somerset House, London, as planner. The forty detached cottages, flanking a wide road edged with grass verges and ascending in gentle curves to the saddle of land below, have whitewashed walls and thatched roofs in a manner characteristic of the local Dorset vernacular.

Inspired though such examples are, however, they did little to stop the rapidly deteriorating social conditions for the rural poor, trapped by low wages, unemployment and rampant inflation.

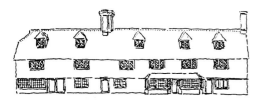

The Walks, Groombridge, Kent. Almost uniform row of early 18th century cottages on high gound at the head of a triangular green. The ground storey is a polychrome of red and blue brick. The upper storey is tile hung.

London's Country and Coast

During the 1630s, the profitable economy of the coastal villages had made them the most affluent areas in this region. By the late 17th century, the improved farming techniques of the yeoman farmer began to enrich the inland villages of the Weald as well. Houses were planned to include parlours while many timber-frame buildings had their plastered walls weather-proofed with tiles or boards.

Tile hanging was rare north of Surrey, Kent and East and West Sussex, and even here it was a luxury before the 17th century. The plain tile is common but decorative patterns were achieved by combining plain tiles with decoratively-shaped tiles. The lightweight

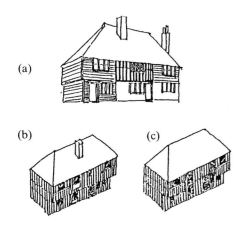

(a)

(b)   (c)

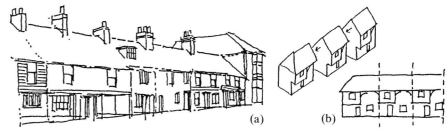

(a)   (b)

Where there was insufficient money for rebuilding along more fashionable lines, many terraces and cottages were simply refronted. This example at Battle, Sussex, consists of nine Wealden houses of the late 16th century, infilled and refronted in the early 18th century. (a) The original terrace plans consisted of a recessed two storey high hall with service rooms to one side. Above, in a jetted bay, was the solar. Such transformation are to be found all over the south east. (b)

Transformation of a Wealden house (or Yeoman's house) into three cottages. (a)There was generally an intermediate stage to such a transformation. The first transformation, taking place in the 17th century, was generally a continuous jettied house. The open hall was given up and joists to carry a floor inserted. In the 18th century the facade itself was replaced along more fashionable lines. (b) and (c).

Right: **Five bay Georgian town house, Lewes.**

Far right: **Georgian house with shallow bay windows, Lewes, Sussex.**

132

timber-framing techniques of south-eastern England in the early 19th century were particularly suited to tile hanging, seen at its best in places such as Groombridge and Lewes. The mathematical tile was developed for the more fashion-conscious. Like plain tiling, it was nailed to wood lathing, but the tile shaped in section to give the appearance of brickwork. It was introduced to the South-East in the mid-18th century and was used well into the 19th century. It was an inexpensive way to make a timber-frame building more fashionable while avoiding the brick taxes. Telltale signs of walling clad with mathematical tiles can be seen in the detailing around windows which usually shows the shallow depth of walling.

In Essex weatherboarding, a covering of overlapping horizontal boards to throw off rain from the walls, had been used to protect windmills and watermills since the 15th century, while from the 16th century onwards, most farm buildings in Kent, East and West Sussex and Surrey were using weatherboarding. But it was not until the development of lightweight timber frame construction in the late 18th century, that it was used for domestic buildings. The finest examples are found in Goudhurst, Tenterden and Cranbrook in Kent. Early weatherboarding pegged to the timber frame was usually made of oak or elm, but later deal, a cheap soft wood, was used nailed to studs.

Further west, in Hertfordshire, Buckinghamshire and Bedfordshire, there are some fine timber buildings, but the belt of limestone and clay, which starts at Portland Bill on the South Coast and runs northeastward through the Cotswold Country and the high parts of Northamptonshire, provided an abundance of magnificant building

Early 19th century, weather-boarded cottages, Fyfield, Essex.

Thatched cottage, Bayham, Sussex. Originally a half-timbered cottage with panels of wattle and daub. The infill panels deteriorated and the timber frame was covered in weatherboarding in the late 18th century.

Weather-boarded house at Biddenden, Kent. It was not until the development of lightweight timber frame construction in the late 18th century that weather-boarding was used on domestic buildings.

The High Street, Tenterden, Kent.
Marvellous piece of Kentish townscape with trees, grass verge and weather-boarded cottages.

133

The Red House, Sevenoaks, Kent. Built in 1686, this seven bay, red brick house epitomises the late 17th century ideal, as Pevsner points out.

Rye, a Cinque Port once washed by the sea, is now marooned in the flatness of the Sussex landscape, the sea a thin line on the horizon. This delightful town, straddling a hill of sandstone rock, has many fine 15th to 18th century terrace houses and cottages. Many of the humbler late 16th and 17th century houses were greatly altered in the 18th century - some with whole new facades, others with elegant bays or finely proportioned sash windows. Here are some typical examples of the Rye townscape.

Abbey Street, Faversham, Kent. Well preserved pre-19th century street, of timber frame and brick-built houses of mainly two storeys, dating between the late 16th and 18th century. Of particular interest is the gently meandering wall and roofscape of terraces, the quality and character of the street developed incrementally over some two hundred years.

materials. During the 17th century stone was still used mainly for the larger houses. A characteristic of this period was the gabled dormer. The dormer had been invented in the Middle Ages as a device for making more headroom within the roof space and in the limestone regions it was built with a gable of stone flush with the facade of the house and in Ashwell, Hertfordshire, with bold rustic pargetting. Many of the poorer houses and cottages in Buckinghamshire were built like the cob houses of Devon but of a while clay known as wichert, usually found about eighteen inches below the surface of the ground. By the late 18th century and early 19th century, the first of the cottage rows or semi-detached cottages were built in places such as Ampthill, Elstow and Great Barford. The two-storey elevations were usually symmetrical, invariably of slight timbers with wattle-and-mud infill, but plastered from the start. By the mid-19th century most of the smaller houses and cottages were built of local bricks.

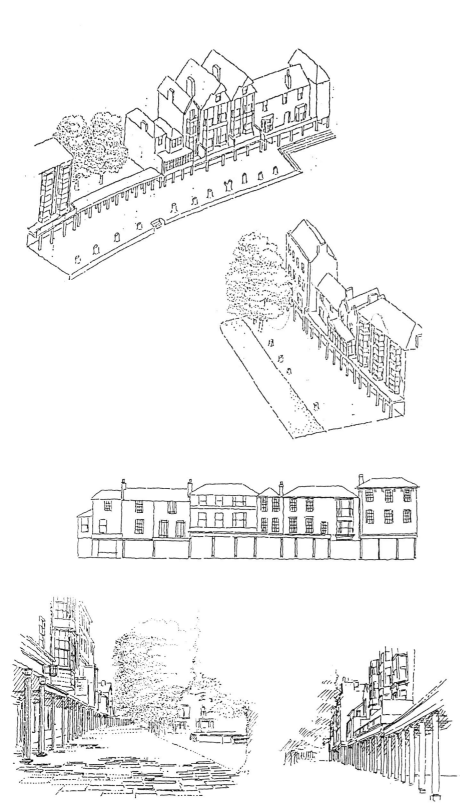

The Pantiles, Tunbridge Wells. Described by Nikolas Pevsner as the perfect pedestrian precinct. Laid out in the mid 17th century, its heyday as a Spa was the early 18th century when the famous dandy, Beau Nash, presided over its entertainments between 1735-1761. Many of the houses are mid 19th century, but the spatial aura is that of the late 18th century. The sense of uniformity is delightfully misleading, the collection of columns, mostly Tuscan, which form the arcade range from some original timber pillars of 1698 to Regency and Early Victorian. The colonnaded shops, aligning the side of a raised walk some 200 yards long, have a gentle curve mirrored by a row of lime trees.

Intriguing structure standing beside the village road at Foxton, Cambridgeshire - an 18th century malthouse, once an integral part of home brewing for the Great House, converted into a cottage in the late 19th century. With its gabled sides, turreted roof and central chimney, it rivals in character the Picturesque's most able rustic conceptions. The intriguing character has come from its very transformation.

Early 19th century cottage of two rooms built at Midville, Lincolnshire.

The lessons for local builders were perfectly clear. For the smaller, Georgian house there was no one better equipped than the local craftsmen to create a simple, symmetrical building, decently proportioned. The example here is of a mid 18th century brick house in Hadleigh, Suffolk. One remarkable aspect of building in the 18th century was how even the design of the smaller house was able to transcend that of the vernacular tradition.

East Anglia and The Fens

The prosperity of East Anglia in the late Middle Ages, based on the flourishing manufacturing revolution created by the Flemish weavers, reached its peak between 1580–1630 when many cottages were built. The typical cottage was a two-roomed plan, the family living in one room, the second being used as a workroom. This basic plan, later provided with an upper chamber, was characteristic of East Anglia and the Fens from the 17th to the 19th century.

Most cottages were brick built, with pantiled roofs, and a gabled parapet to prevent the pantiles or thatch from being lifted by the severe winds typical of this part of the country. A 'tumbled in' gable end, which, without adding a coping or covering on top of the wall, was the smoothest way to finish a straight gable.

18th century Norfolk played a large part in the Agricultural Revolution. Corn used to be sown by throwing handfulls of seed on the ploughed land. This was wasteful as much seed was eaten by birds; it was unevenly sown and strips had to be weeded by hand. Jethro Tull (1674–1741), believing that a field would not need to be left fallow one year in three if the soil was ploughed and hoed while the crops were growing, invented a horsedrawn hoe and a seed drill. This meant that the seed was buried and the corn grew in even rows enabling the ground to be hoed in order to kill the weeds. Crop production was doubled with only a third of the seed but this method was little used until the 19th century.

Above left: Semi-detatched cottages built in Lincolnshire, 1793. Because of the severity of winds in this part of the country, it was the tradition to take the gables up above the level of the roof to prevent thatch or tile being lifted.

Above right: Late 18th century brick cottage with pantile roof at Stradsett, Norfolk. Note the parapet wall and 'tumble in' gable end.

The new method for sowing and cultivating crops required large-scale farming, and by the mid-18th century the enclosure movement in East Anglia was in full swing. In the open village the married labourer would often build his own cottage, unlike the unmarried labourer who would be housed in the parlour or garret of his employer. In some cases dormers were added to the mansard roofs. In the closed villages the building was developed by the landlord himself.

The land was, by now, sufficiently well drained and farmers began to develop way of revolutionizing the agricultural economy. The Flemish farmers had been intensively cultivating their poor sandy soils since the Middle Ages. Their now flourishing commercial farms gave inspiration to the English farmer. The soils of East Anglia were equally thin and infertile. In 1778 Coke of Holkham began farming on this poor soil. By digging the underlying marl and spreading it over the sandy top soil he was able to convert it into rich cornland. He adopted the four year rotation developed by Charles Townshend whereby

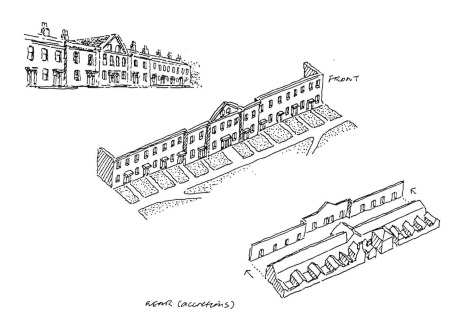

FRONT

REAR (accretions)

The idea of creating a unified composition out of a row of houses became fashionable in the late 18th and early 19th century, whether in the major urban centres or smaller country towns. In the former, the terrace and associated open space might take the form of some monumental palace; in the latter pretension was lent to medium size houses by giving the whole composition the aura of a palatial country mansion. As Stefan Muthesius points out in *The English Terraced House,* this type of terrace " ...became so fashionable for a time around 1800 that a house within it seemed preferable to even a good-sized detached villa. One can thus find tightly grouped terraces of medium size not just in denser areas, but also in the leafy outer suburbs of provincial towns, placed in large semi-private parks." The terrace in Newmarket Road, Norwich, illustrated here, he quotes as an example. Built early 19th century.

Typical romanticized estate cottage, early 19th century, Sudbourne, Suffolk. Unlike the vernacular around, this was not *real* character, but merely the *idea* of character. The character, unlike that of the vernacular, was formed not by functional determinants, but primarily by aesthetic predelictions.

137

Medieval weavers' houses, Kersey, Suffolk. Like Lavenham, the wealth of medieval timber frame houses was such that any expansion over the centuries was accommodated by outshuts or by extending wings, or adding an additional bay. Some houses had their timber plastered over, in some, old casement windows were replaced by sliding sash windows. Where possible, use was made of the old - some larger houses aligning the winding village street were subdivided in the 18th and early 19th centuries into smaller cottage units. It is this series of rather ad hoc accretions that has given Kersey such charm — a medieval core, or frame, with 18th and 19th century touches.

A characteristic plan of the early 18th century farmhouse was what is known as the double-pile house. For the larger house, the most convenient form of structure was to put, in principle, two houses back to back, each with its own roof and gabled chimney, the roof joined by a valley gutter. This plan, which was the precursor of those throughout the 18th century, provided a central passage and stair giving independent access to each room on the ground and first floors. This example is at Brechfa, Carmarthenshire, built in 1724.

turnips were cultivated one year, then barley, clover and wheat. Encouraged by the low corn prices, expanding markets and the conversion of some arable land to pasture, the Norfolk four-course, as it was known, was well established by the turn of the 19th century.

But the Norfolk system required more labour and this labour force had to be housed. The agricultural economy was prosperous and the landowner could, therefore, afford to develop more radical solutions to the problems of housing. This resulted in model villages like the estate village of Holkham (1760s) built in a superior Tudor-style of semi-detached and detached cottages lining the entrance to the park gates. But the model village was not new. Some, like Chippenham (1702) in Cambridgeshire, were more a product of emparking when an existing village was swallowed up by the new park and lake, and a new village built nearby. In 1729 Sir Robert Walpole built two rows of cottages, almhouses and two farmhouses at the gates of his mansion, Houghton Hall. The cottages were spacious and outside each a strip of land was provided for cultivation. The improved housing standards of such housing estates were a lesson to all, but few landowners followed suit.

Wales

There were lead mines in Cardiganshire and Dyfed and small industries scattered here and there in South Wales but, like their forefathers, most people lived directly off the land. Free entry to the English market had encouraged the development of a flourishing trade. The sheep on the uplands produced the wool, while the textile industry developed the cloth for export. There was a thriving trade in corn and dairy products but the major industry was provided by the black cattle of Dyfed and the western counties that were driven into England for sale. As London and the Midland cities grew, the cattle became of prime importance to Wales. Vast herds were driven along the mountain tracks across the border with England, the herdsmen bringing back much needed cash.

A characteristic of the pastoral economy was the simpler circular or rectangular huts, called hafod. Usually no more than ten feet in diameter, they resembled the round houses of the Iron Age Celts. Herds and flocks were moved from the valley in the spring to feed in the mountain pastures. The family, or part of it, would take up summer residence in these simple upland dwellings. Furniture was usually made of stones; the fire was situated at the end with a smoke hole in the roof above. The enclosures in the late 18th century, the growth of sheep farming to supply the wool for looms during the Industrial Revolution and the development of more permanent farms ended the summer migrations.

Typical thatch-roofed cottages, Plas Coch, Rhoscolyn.

18th century cottage at Llangorwen, Cardiganshire. Entry is beside the fireplace in the gable end. The projecting window bay is of a later date.

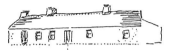

18th century range of cottage and farm buildings, Llanrug, Powys. Originally only the cottage was built. The farm buildings were added later. Such accretions were typical of 18th and 19th century Wales, particularly where small holdings were concerned.

Characteristic of Dyfed, Carmarthenshire and Cardiganshire were houses built of cob or stone and constructed with rounded corners. They were often framed with scarfed or jointed crucks and then covered with a light thatched roof. The roof was finished in a half hip while the fireplace hood, chimney and partitions were built of clay-daubed wickerwork. The walls of the house were normally colour washed in red, pink or ochre, while the farm buildings themselves were white.

The big boom in cottage building began in the mid-18th century with the break up of the simple pastoral economy by the Industrial Revolution. The enclosures drove the poor to carve small homesteads out of the inferior soil of the mountains and moors. It was the growth of industry that saved Wales from catastrophe. The country was virtually isolated; the roads were poor and the landowners had little capital to invest in new industry. The money and expertise to expand quarrying, mining, metalworking and textile manufacturing arrived from England. The abundance of new jobs not only absorbed the labour force of Wales, but attracted a flock of immigrants from England.

Many of the new cottages were founded in scattered semi-rural settlements where miners and quarrymen could supplement their earnings by small-scale farming. These cottages fall into two distinct groups. The first adopted the traditional storeyed house of the poor. They had high-pitched roofs, suitable for thatch and small, irregularly-placed windows. Partitions were rudimentary, often made of cloth or

Cottage at Beddgelert, Gwynedd, 1791. This type of cottage, with entry positioned away from the gable ended fireplace, is characteristic of north-west and south-west Wales.

Combination of house and byre. This example in Llanfynydd, Gwynedd of the late 17th century, has an entrance to the house via the byre. This 'longhouse' tradition continued well into the 18th century.

Some farmhouses of the 18th century consisted of a single pile house with extra accommodation provided in an outshut to the rear. This example, at Trefdraeth, Anglesey, was built in 1731.

Pennant, travelling through Wales in 1773-6 described the houses of the common people as being " ...made with clay, thatched, and destitute of chimneys." So insubstantial were they that few exist before the 18th century. According to Peter Smith, the great age of cottage building in Wales is the mid 18th to mid 19th century. Typical is this three unit cottage at Trefeglwys, Powys.

The Old Royal Oak (Cynwyl Gaco, Carmarthenshire) built in the late 18th century.

wisps of straw. Some were able to afford a dresser or a tiered cupboard which was placed where it would serve as a division so that the parlour could be screened off from the entrance. The second group was built primarily in the Industrial Revolution. Roof pitches were lower as slate replaced thatch, windows were larger and more regularly spaced and partitions were of lath and plaster on studded walls or of matchboard or masonry.

The structure of the house was changing. The cottage along the industrial areas of the north east adopted the lightweight timber construction of Kent and Sussex. Walls were made either of weatherboarding or of lath and plaster. Elsewhere cottages were built of mass construction. The design and construction of the earliest industrial housing in Wales, however, followed pretty closely the pattern of traditional building, the factory owner leaving decisions about planning and construction to local builders. Some, like the terraces beside the site of the furnaces at Gellideg, Merthyr Tydfil, Glamorgan, were additions to earlier buildings. Built in 1769, the earliest part was originally a farmhouse before the ironworks were founded. The successive additions, of seven, two storey terraces, transformed the stepped row from a rural building to terraces for industrial workers.

Stack Square and Engine Row, Blaenavon, Gwent, is one of the earliest industrial settlements to be found here. Built between 1789 and 1792, the houses are quite conventional: two rooms on each floor and a larder and built with traditional construction of stone walls, oak beams and timber partitions inside. By standards of the time they were quite spacious, varying from 44 to 57 square metres in area. What was

Timber framed cottage, Llanfechain, Montgomeryshire.

Two roomed timber-framed 18th century cottage with a lobby entrance along the gable end beside the fireplace. Forden, Powys.

Early 18th century farmhouse, Mochdre, Montgomeryshire. The timber frame house stands on a stone base built on sloping ground, allowing room for a basement at the lower end below the parlour.

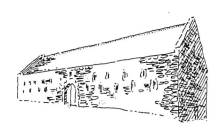

A remnant of the 17th century, a great stone-built corn barn built in 1685 at Llanddwywe-is-y-graig, Merioneth.

unique was the overall plan, consisting of two parallel rows of terraces enclosed on a third side by a range of buildings originally accommodating the company shop and administrative offices. The company works were only 100 metres away.

Despite the partial mechanization of some of the earliest lead mines, such as that at Cwmystwyth, Dyfed, in the late 18th century, the workers still lived in crofts and cottages where they were able to supplement their income by working the land. In the North and West Wales a characteristic house is the one-storey, two-roomed house built from the mid-18th century onwards by the peasant farmers and farm workers. This house type was a pattern adapted for housing the workers in the mining and quarrying areas of the west. They were usually built in blocks of three and used rather like barracks to house workers, who were living too far off, from Monday to Friday night.

In Bunkers Hill, Bersham, Clywd, is another early row of industrial housing. The long row of single storey houses built end to end in 1785 and constructed of brick with steeply pitched roofs, consisted of two rooms, and are similar to those found in West Wales. These house types, with a steep pitched roof more suited to pantiles, were in fact designs imported by John Wilkinson, the iron master, from the Shropshire coal-fields where they were comparatively characteristic.

Back to back housing was developed in the industrial towns of the Midlands and Yorkshire from the 1790s. It was not long before such terraces were built in the industrial centres of Wales for, amongst other things, they were extremely economic in the use of building materials. There was a good example in Bunkers Row, Blaenavon, built in 1792, consisting of twenty houses of one ground floor room with loft above. The row was demolished in 1872.

141

It was comparatively simple to transform the domestic timber frame buildings. There was sufficient local labour and skill. This late 15th century cottage in Stottesden, Shropshire, was converted into two cottages in the early 19th century.

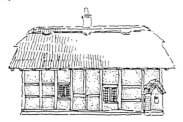

The proliferation of timber frame buildings in Worcester is due entirely to the scarcity, and hence expense, of stone as a building material. This 18th century structure at Abbots Morton, Worcestershire, started life off as a barn, later converted into a cottage, and finally a post office.

Decorative use of brickwork in an eaves cornice of a cottage in Barsby, Leicestershire, in 1701. A cornice of uncut brick divides the two floors.

142

Another terrace type for industrial housing was the dual row, built from the 1790s onward, and consisting of a row of houses built in a stepped section along a parallel ridge of land allowing for a basement row excavated in the hillside and reached from the lower ground, with an entirely separate row built above and reached from the higher ground. A good example was built in Nantyglo, Gwent in 1793 to house the workers in the ironworks of Harford and Company.

The Midlands

In the late 17th and early 18th centuries, many farmers were involved in fattening cattle brought down from Wales and Scotland for the London market. And of course the growth of industry in Lancashire, Yorkshire, the Black Country, the North Midlands and the north east coast, provided alternative markets for the farmer. The development by Abraham Darby in 1709 of a method of smelting iron by coke rather than charcoal and the successful experiments with high-pressure steam by Richard Trevithick during the 1790s, resulted in the removal of the iron industry from Sussex to the Black Country in the West Midlands.

The upland areas were given over to sheep to meet the ever increasing demand of the cloth-producing centres, while mutton provided a staple diet for the Durham and Northumberland miners. Throughout the North Midlands the land was given over to wheat, barley and oats.

Brick houses, which first appeared in the East Midlands in the early 17th century, became more common. Timber-framed buildings were sometimes given a brick facade. Many of the poorer buildings in Northamptonshire were still being built of earth walls, mainly one-and-a-half storeys in height. Some were built of poor crucks. Methods had changed little in this part of the region by the beginning of the 19th century.

The major roads in the deep clays of the Midlands and the Home Counties where soft going had long obstructed traffic, were now improved by the introduction of turnpikes in the 18th century which collected tolls for the maintenance of the roads. The fattening areas of the Midlands were one of the main goals of the cattle drovers. After the Act of Union in 1707 Scottish cattle were driven down either side of the Pennines to Lincolnshire, Leicestershire and East Anglia. The Welsh tradition goes back to the Middle Ages. The chief route from South and Central Wales for the drovers was through Hereford and Worcetser, and the towns of Ross-on-Wye, Ledbury and Tewkesbury to the South Midland grasslands. From North Wales they went through Bromwich and Warwickshire in the direction of Barnet Fair, the Essex grazings and the London butchers. But they kept to the lanes and byways rather than pay tolls on the main roads. Today their routes are marked by the old Drovers' Inn.

While the more advanced and flexible agricultural methods of mid-18th century Norfolk and the eastern counties were not affected by the low grain prices between 1730 and 1750, the open-field system of the Midlands, too rigid to adapt, suffered. Eventually improved cropping systems were adopted. Land that could not be tilled was given over to grass for dairying and for fattening the large numbers of lean stock brought into Leicestershire and the Central Midlands from Wales and Scotland. Outbreaks of animal disease, bad winters and periodical harvest failures in the early 18th century weeded out many of the small farmers who were subsequently bought out by the larger farms. In the West and Central Midlands, particularly in Leicestershire, Warwickshire and Northamptonshire, the act of enclosure tended to extend the area already under grass and by the mid-18th century there was considerably less farming in the Midlands. The unemployed labourers flocked to the new industrial centres now being opened up by the canals and railways. Large stocking mills were developed at Belper in Derbyshire. Near the mills terraced houses were built for the new workers. But there was considerable difference between working in their own homes under the dual economy of domestic weaving and working in a factory. Conditions were hard with long hours, poor light and monotonous work.

By the late 18th century Wedgwood, Spode, Minton and Copeland with the ready supply of raw material and new markets, had made great technical advances, and they soon firmly established the pottery

Early 18th century house at Yazor, Hereford and Worcester. Timber frame house, with brick panelling, built on a stone base. Good example of small framing.

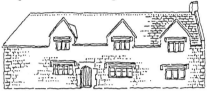

House built of coursed rubble at Honeybourne, Hereford and Worcester, in the late 17th century.

Characteristic cottage of the Severn Valley of the late 18th and early 19th century, is a simple one or two room cottage with a large chimney built at the gable end.

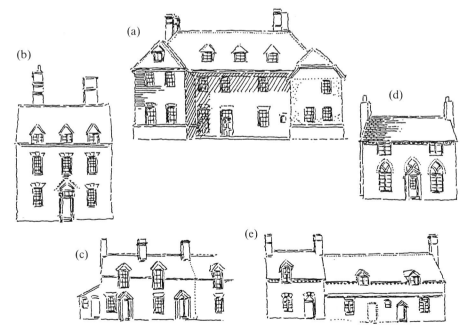

Jackfield, Coalbrookdale, is a small industrial community running along the River Severn. More good examples of small industrial housing, as well as some slightly grander houses of the late 17th century to mid 18th century.
(a) The Tuckies, Jackfield, c.1698. Seven bay brick house with projecting wings.
(b) The Calcotts, Jackfield, 1695. Three bay, red brick house with attic storey lit by dormers.
(c) Range of cottages, Jackfield, 1750.
(d) Primrose Cottage, Jiggers Bank, Jackfield.
(e) Nos.44-46 Wellington Road, Jackfield.

143

Blacksmith's Cottage, late 17th century, Oughton, Warwickshire. The forge adjoins the cottage to the left.

Cottages, Broadway, Hereford and Worcester. There are many fine late 17th and 18th century houses and cottages here. Of particular interest is this example of the combination of entrance porch and projecting window bay under one stone slated hood.

There are several fine cottages in the main street at Barsby, Leicestershire. This, the most interesting, dates from 1691. The first floor has a diaper-pattern of black headers, the ground floor a chequer pattern. The two floors are separated by a purposed moulded-brick cornice.

Manor House, Woodnewton, Northamptonshire, c. 1730. Extraordinary composition. Five bay house, with three storey central projecting section of three bays with 1½ storey high flanking bays. The front facade, with its split and inter-penetrating pediments, is thought to be based on a formula of Hawksmoor and Archer, according to Kerry Downes.

Brizlincote Hall, Burton-on-Trent, 1714. Another extraordinary composition - a house crowned by enormous segmental pediments on all four sides.

industry on the clays of Tunstall, Burslem, Hanley, Stoke, Fenton and Longton. By the end of that century James Brindley's ambitious scheme to provide continuous waterways from coast to coast, the Grand Trunk Canal, was completed.

Stone replaced timber buildings for some of the smaller houses and cottages by the late 18th century and early 19th century. In parts of Hereford and Worcester and typical Cotswold detail of the ground floor bay window combined with the entrance door under the same stone slated hood can be seen. The gabled end of the roof and the sides to many gabled dormers were timber framed with panels of wattle and daub. Windows and doors had elabroate drip-mouldings to protect the head and returns of the opening below. Occasionally a simple projection was provided, or, as in Northamptonshire, the stone lintel was more common. Thatch was still a common roofing material, but in the East and Central Midlands it was eventually replaced by the pantile. In Derbyshire, Northamptonshire and the borderlands with Wales, stone slates are common. Many came from the quarries at Stonesfield in Oxfordshire or Collyweston in Northamptonshire.

Increasingly manufacturing moved from the domestic system to the factory. In 1762 Matthew Boulton set up his factory by the Birmingham Canal for metal manufacture. The evolution of the invention of the rotary motion by Watt, which was patented in 1781, made possible the age of steam. But for the new factory workers, still countrymen at heart, conditions were hard, their freedoms gone.

The Industrial North and The Moors

Many of the 18th century smallholders still lived in a dwelling known in Yorkshire as a *coit*. This building type consisted of domestic quarters combined under one roof with the barn or shippon. It was usually built for one of the farm labourers on the larger farms. The span of the roof was carried on four wooden pillars; the shippon would usually contain stalls for cattle divided from the threshing floor by a heck over which the animals could be fed. House and shippon had their own external doors, but in bad weather the labourer would use a connecting door between the two by which to feed the cattle.

The traditional hall, in use during the 17th century, was gradually transformed, by the separation of byre from domestic quarters, and by providing a chamber in the roof. A variation of the traditional longhouse was also developed. Built for the larger farms in the remoter uplands of Lancashire and Yorkshire in the mid-18th century, it consisted of a fairly spacious two storey house built in one range with a barn. The barn usually had an upper level opening into the loft.

With the growth of the cloth in the mid-17th century, and the need too for some kind of dual economy to keep above subsistance level, weaving became a common industry in the living rooms of the small farmhouse and cottages as in other parts of the country. But even then many smallholdings failed. The gentry or larger farmer began to expand their farms in the upland country of Yorkshire. They had the capital and now they had the land with which to increase hay production.

Late 18th century weavers' cottage, West Yorkshire. The cottage, built of millstone grit, has a loom shop on the first floor. The multiple lights, back and front, were designed to let in the maximum light. Some existing houses were converted, either with the roof space being turned into a weaving loft, or a new, two storey extension might be added.

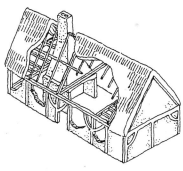

As Eric Mercer has pointed out in *English Vernacular Houses,* some late 17th and early 18th century houses in parts of Lincolnshire, Nottinghamshire, Lancashire and North Yorkshire, were built of mud and stud, often on a brick plinth. Generally they had low lofts used for storage. Conditions were hard and to keep above subsistence level a cottager needed to be involved in some kind of dual economy. The growth of the cloth industry from the mid 17th century provided the possibility for supplementing an otherwise meagre living.

Stone walled house with pedimented central section, built 1715 at Sowerby Bridge, West Yorkshire.

145

Lovely five bay stone-built house with pedimented front, built c.1730-50 at Colne, Lancashire. The attic storey is lit by the mullioned window in the pedimented gable.

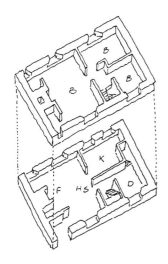

Late 17th or early 18th century farmhouse, Samlesbury, Lancashire. It is a small stone-built house. The lobby entrance at the end of one side is typical of many houses built in the north at this time. A new and widespread feature is the closet to the side of the fireplace on the first floor.

Aisled barn with sleeping quarters at one end, built in 1689 at Dalton, Lancashire.

In the Bradford area many weavers began to move their looms upstairs. By the late 17th century the parlour was added to many house plans. Although it had sitting room furniture, it was used here as a parlour bedroom, a characteristic of the north. The most common building material for the poor had been wattle and daub, but by the early 17th century the inclement climate of the moorlands and mountain districts necessitated a stronger material and so, where possible, stone was used. In Yorkshire, where an abundance of large blocks was available, walls eighteen inches to two feet thick were invariably built of roughly-squared stones, laid with some attempt at coursing. The stones were left dry outside with rubble, sand or clay as an internal filling. In the Isle of Man many buildings were built of unquarried stone. Often the walls would be plastered or whitewashed over. The roof would be made of thatch or thick stone plates. But the stone buildings of the north are more austere and utilitarian than those in the pure limestone country of the Cotswolds. Most are built of red sandstone or a millstone grit from the Pennines. Chimneys are usually square, often with short, rounded stacks. In Humberside, where the only available material was limestone or millstone rubble, sandstone was used for quoins and for window dressings and doorheads. In the upland areas stone slates replaced thatch for roofing while in the flatter districts of Yorkshire and Humberside, particularly the eastern edge of the Vale of York, pantiles were used as a replacement for thatch in the 19th century.

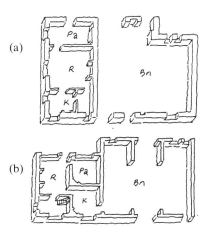

(a)

(b)

Plan of laithe houses at Dinckley, Lancashire. (a) Todmorden, West Yorkshire. (b) The laithe house combines a dwelling and a barn under one roof. The combination of barn and byre is the laithe. Separate doorways lead to the house and laithe. sometimes the two may be connected. Late 18th century and early 19th century laithe houses were built by smallholders farming recently-enclosed or divided lands on the fringes of the moors.

Before the re-organisation and subsequent concentration of industry in the towns, the domestic systems in the clothing industry carried out by workmen and their families at home predominated. The merchants collected the wool, took it to the spinners and later collected the yarn they had spun. This was then taken to the weaver's cottage to be turned into cloth. Most weavers' houses, both in the town and country, consisted of a work room for the looms either in a first floor room or a loft space. The rooms were lit by a long row of

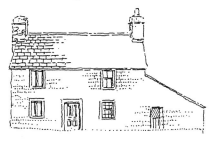

18th century cottage built of rubble walling with a stone slate roof. The outshut to the right is a later extension. To the left was a range of rubble walled farm buildings. The house itself was whitewashed to make it more distinctive.

18th century range of house and barn, Horton, West Yorkshire.

147

Aisled barn and byre with a house at one end. Built in the 18th century at Old Laund Booth, Lancashire.

Characteristic house of the late 17th century, Appleton-le-Moors, Yorkshire.

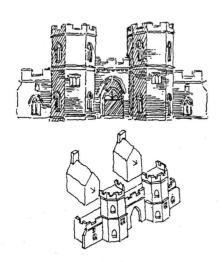

What at first appears to be a decorative gatehouse is really a combination of Gothic folly and Farmhouse - castellated Gothic front facade with more utilitarian structure containing main rooms and service rooms to the rear - built c.1790 at Sledmore, North Humberside.

windows, while some of the lights opened to ventilate the workroom. Sometimes there was a separate access by an external staircase. The more well-to-do weaver often had a separate workshop attached to a conventional house.

But many of the smallholders supplementing their living by weaving, were hard hit by the Industrial Revolution. As weaving increasingly moved from the domestic to the factory system so the small freeholders, tenant farmers and commoners were taken over by the large corn-growing and meat-producing farms. The expanding industries needed workers and the workers needed feeding, and this market could only be met by the bigger and more progressive farms.

The Weaver Navigation Scheme, and the construction of the Bridgewater and Sankey Canals, liberated the north for industrial expansion. In 1764 Hargreaves invented a machine, the Spinning Jenny, for spinning eight threads at once. In 1769 Arkwright invented the water frame. Crompton then improved on the two by inventing the spinning mule which revolutionized the textile industry. For the first time both spinning and weaving could be done in factories. Machines were installed, powered first by water and later by steam.

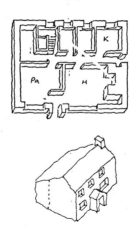

Plan characteristic of a late 17th or early 18th century house in West Yorkshire. The rear part of the house was built as a continuous range in an outshut. It is a development from the traditional aisled hall, the house of the 12th century nobility, such as Oakham Castle, Leicestershire.

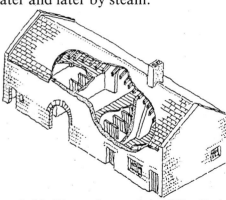

Laithe House, characteristic of West Yorkshire in the late 18th century. The early longhouses were the houses of men at a very low economic level, with provision for a few animals. The laithe house was a product of the hilly country bordering the industrial areas of West Yorkshire. The considerable influence of the small holders here by 1700 was based on the increasing market for their dairy products, as well as a supplementary income from the 'putting out' system of the woollen industry. The laithe house was a combination of barn and byre, and the barn was as important as the byre, unlike in the longhouse. A prominent feature was a high arched entrance into the laithe to allow a loaded hay-sled to pass beneath. Diagram based on a study of the laithe house by Eric Mercer.

148

Northumberland and The Lakes

The manorial customs of the Lake District, in which farms were handed down through the family, meant that most farmhouses were carefully rebuilt or extended. But by the 18th century inflation, mortgage debts and a variety of other problems resulted in many farms changing hands. The characteristic farmhouse plan of this period was long range consisting of a central house finished in rough cast and limewashed in contrast to the dry-stone walling of the range of farm buildings built on either side of the house.

Roof pitches were altered to give headroom in the loft space for bedrooms. Storm porches designed to keep out the winds were added; a new entrance opened up and a through passage created, separating the living quarters from the byre. Some farms had a separate barn or byre built some distance away but at right angles to the main building.

Most buildings here in the 18th century were small, even for the yeoman farmer. It was a poor region; few farmers used labour outside the family and so fewer cottages were found. Most cottages were single storey with only two rooms. The typical plan consisted of a kitchen-living room, a fireplace on the gable wall and a small parlour-bedroom. The entrance door was positioned centrally at the front with a window either side to light the living room and the parlour. By the mid-18th century a two-storey cottage, based on a similar ground floor plan, was common. A narrow staircase or companion-way ladder concealed in a cupboard, led to the upper floor bedrooms. The single-fronted houses, with one up and one down, was a smaller version of this. Many of these were developed in short rows or terraces.

Gradually roads were made, the moorlands drained, woods planted and the wastelands enclosed. In the late 18th century half of Northumberland was still waste land but by the 19th century much of this waste land had been transformed by extensive cultivation.

Early 19th century terraces, of limestone walls and pantiled roofs, Piercebridge, County Durham.

Stone walled miners terraces built in the village of Blanchland, Northumberland, in the 18th century. The model village, marooned in wild moorland, was begun in 1752 by the Earl of Crewe to house workers from the local mines.

(a)

(b)

(c)

The 17th century vernacular legacy was a series of simple, stone-built houses. Some, as in this house at Low Hartsop, Patterdale, Cumbria (a), had distinctive round chimneys. The house at Thrangholm, Dalston, Cumbria (b), was a distinctly more elaborate affair, built of red sandstone rubble with grey sandstone dressings. This simple and dramatically austere building tradition of this region continued well into the 18th century as the terraces at Askham, Westmoreland (c), demonstrate.

149

Numerous model villages were built, but the most interesting was Lowther Village, Cumbria, begun in the 1760s. Sir James Lowther commissioned the Adam brothers to design the village as a model community. Planned on a grand scale, complete with central arc and flanked by squares in the form of a Greek cross, only two closes were built, consisting of two and single storey stone built terraces designed in an austere vernacular style.

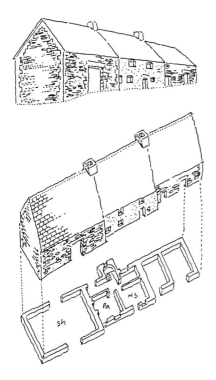

View of a farm range at Brow Edge, Haverthwaite, Cumbria. The central house is finished in rough cast and limewashed in contrast to the dry-stone walling of the range of farm buildings built on either side of the house. Typical of farm buildings from the 18th century onwards.

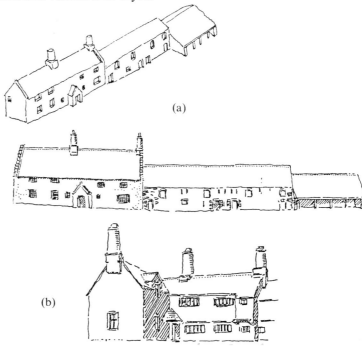

(a)

(b)

Example of 17th century statesmen's houses in Cumbria, (a) Glencoyne farmhouse, Patterdale (b) House, Townend near Troutbeck.

Typical stone walled cottages, Co. Durham.

The Scottish Lowlands and Border Country

In the late 18th century many of the poorer households still lived in cruck-framed turf houses. In parts of Stirlingshire, now in Central Region, many such houses were constructed not by building up walls of cut turf or peat, but by carving away the surrounding ground leaving only the solid walls of the house. Most turf walls were built up on a foundation of rubble. Some examples survived until about 1860 on Redding Muir and at March End, Polmont in Central Region and another example was found as recently as 1920 at Torbrex, near St Ninians in the same region.

Other materials most readily available were clay and stone. Both were used in the construction of loadbearing and non-loadbearing walls. In Stirlingshire the slightly better-off were able to afford buildings built of clay, tempered with chopped straw as a foundation for rough stone. The walls were non-loadbearing, the roof loads being distributed by cruck trusses to the stone footings. But by the late 18th and early 19th centuries many of these houses were gradually replaced by dwellings built of more substantial materials. In Ruthwell, in Dumfries and Galloway in south west Scotland, all the houses were built originally in clay, but the *Old Statistical Account of 1792* describes how many clay houses were rebuilt with stone and slated, and the streets of the village widened and laid in a straight line. Yet at Hutton in Borders Region and Corrie in Strathclyde, people were still living in clay-built houses by the mid-19th century. The clay walling in Scotland was a less painstaking and lengthy task than the cob walling in Devon. In Devon it would take several months to build a cob-walled

Weavers' cottages built on a sloping site at Kilbarchan, Renfrew. Advantage was taken of the sloping site to make an additional room above the weaving shop.

18th century house, Castlegate, Jedburgh.

Adencaple House, Seil. A laird's small house of the late 18th century. A symmetrically-planned building with a turnpike staircase built out in a semi-circular bay at the rear.

Early 18th century house, originally Manor Inn, Lanton. The pebble masonary walls were harled, the ashlar surrounds to the openings were left exposed.

Illustration from Thomas Pennant's *A Tour in Scotland and Voyage to the Hebrides*, **1774, showing typical huts or shielings erected in Jura.**

18th century house, Town Yetholm, Roxburgh-shire.

Late 18th century thatched roof cottage with harled rubble walls, Town Yetholm, Roxburgh-shire.

18th century house, Kirk Yetholm.

18th century house, remodelled in the mid 19th century as a court-house and prison, Bolgam Street, Campbeltown.

18th century houses in the Market Place, Selkirk. The houses are pebble walled, and the walls rendered with only the quoins and window surrounds left exposed

house but in Dumfries and Galloway, as in Cumbria across the border, walls tended to be built in a day as a communal venture, possibly for a newly-married couple or for elderly people. The late 18th century account from the Dumfries parish of Dornock is interesting:

"The farmhouses in general, and all the cottages, are built of mud or clay; yet these houses, when plastered and properly finished within are exceedingly warm and comfortable. The manner of erecting them is singular. In the first place, they dig out the foundation of the house, and lay a row or two of stones, then they procure from a pit contiguous, as much clay or brick earth as is sufficient to form the walls and having provided a quantity of straw, or other litter to mix with the clay, upon a day appointed, the whole neighbourhood, male and female, to the number of twenty or thirty, assemble, each with a dung fork, a spade or some such instrument. Some fall to the working of the clay or mud, by mixing it with straw; others carry the materials; and four or six of the most experienced hands, build and take care of the walls. In this manner the walls of the house are finished in a few hours, after which, they retire to a good dinner and plenty of drink which is provided for them, where they have music and a dance, with which, and other marks of festivity, they conclude the evening. This is called a 'daubing' and in this manner they made a frolic of what could otherwise be a very dirty and disagreeable job."

The walls were built in courses on a stone foundation or footing which acted as damp-proof course. In parts of Berwickshire in the Borders Region small stones were mixed with the clay to form a very hard durable material. Despite the quickness of the building process timber shutting was rarely used in south west Scotland, but in the south east a system known as cat and clay was common. Here the walls were constructed of bunches of straw mixed with soft clay and packed into a wooden framework of upright and cross spars. Many of these clay houses, particularly in Berwickshire, were roofed in pantiles, but a covering of straw-and-clay thatch laid over sods was common in Fife and the Kyle and Carrick District of Strathclyde. A characteristic of the Kilmarnock area in this region in the late 18th century was a method of thatching with straw and mortar. Thatching was carried out in the usual manner, a mortar mixed with cut straw was then thinly spread over the thatch with a large trowel. Clay thatching was thought a considerable improvement over the more common roped thatch. The floors of the houses were often made of clay, sometimes with a decorative strip of whitening round the edges.

In the 18th century fireplaces were still in an open hearth in the centre of the kitchen floor. A wide canopied chimney made of wattle and daub was hung over the fire. By the turn of the 19th century the central hearth was being replaced by chimneys built either as a projecting canopy or as an enclosed stone-built flue built on the end walls of the houses.

In the rural areas the longhouse tradition of byre, stable and living quarters under one roof was typical of most farmhouses. The solid

Early 18th century terraces to house the slate-workers at Ballachulish, Strathclyde.

Residence of a tacksman, Cara, Strathclyde, built in 1733 of rubble masonary laid in lime mortar.

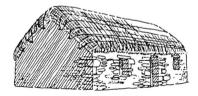

Dalriadic type of black house, typical of the Strathclyde Region.

Group of thatch-roofed houses, Town Yetholm, Roxburghshire.

153

Typical cottages at Morebattle Village, Ingleside, Roxburghshire.

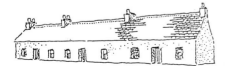

One of a group of three cottages, in the village of Tayinloan. Simple rubble walled cottage with central entrance, built 1755.

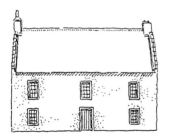

A characteristic house of the early 18th century was a three bay, two storey house with a central entrance, two rooms per floor flanking the central corridor and stair with chimneys on each gable end. This example is in Falkland, Fife. Such houses were built for the merchants of the coastal ports, tacksmen, farmers and the rising middle class.

cross wall separating the byre from the living quarters was rare but a light partition of wattle and daub was typical. In the old county of Ayrshire, now in Strathclyde Region, it was still customary in the early 19th century for the cattle and family to enter the house by the same entrance. Later the byre was built separately and the old byre converted into an additional living room. The solid cross wall became typical, often with a fireplace and chimney built in. The entrance door was usually in the centre of the long wall.

Living conditions for labourers in Roxburgh, in Borders Region, in the mid-18th century were deplorable. Most houses were built of cat and clay. The walls were usually no more than approximately five feet high. Windows were small and few. Most houses were thatched. In Selkirk the Minister of Galashiels wrote in 1797:

"Farmhouses are in general paultry and ill built. Most of the dwelling houses are of one storey, low in the roof, badly lighted and covered with thatch. The walls, however, are of stone and lime; and of late a few of these low houses have been slated . . . the cottages . . . are wretched habitations, dark, smoky and insufficient defences against wind and rain."

In Stirlingshire many of the farm-tenants had to provide their own accommodation. The Reverend Patrick Graham, writing in the late 18th century, described some of these:

" . . . the houses of the peasantry were wretched huts, thatched with

154

Two roomed 18th century cottage built of harled rubble, Lilliesleaf, Roxburgh.

fern or straw, having two apartments, only, the one a kitchen . . . the other a sort of room . . . where strangers were occasionally received, and where the heads of the family generally slept. The byre and stable were generally under the same roof, and separated from the kitchen by a partition of osiers wrought upon slender wooden posts, and plastered with clay. A glass window and a chimney were esteemed a luxury, and were seldom met with."

By the end of the 18th century the farmer and his labourers, but rarely the shepherd, were living in better conditions. The new farmhouse, for the most part two storeys in height with a garret in the roof, usually formed one side of a farm court. They were oblong in shape, about 40 feet by 21 feet containing five rooms with additional accommodation for servants in the lofts. Under the agrarian reformers of the late 18th century many tenants were rehoused in stone-built houses with roofs covered in slate or pantiles. The one-storey cottages of the married labourers were much improved. Walls were about seven feet high and the floor was more often of flags or timber than earth. The roof was usully thatched but accommodation might include a kitchen, a bedroom for children and a garret. The theory behind such improvements was not entirely philanthropic. These improvements had to be paid for but the argument was put forward that well-housed tenants made better farmers than poorly-housed ones and so the expected higher profits would easily cover such developments. The architectural pattern books and agricultural journals were full of useful hints. Bricks were seldom used unless the laird, as in the Paxton

(a)

(b)   (c)

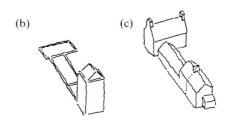

Curious collection of buildings - (a) outbuildings and farmhouse incorporating a late 16th century tower, Flemington. The tower, originally three storeys high, was incorporated in the farm buildings built c.1712 (b) and (c).

155

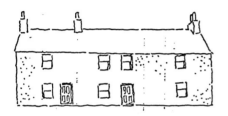

Clovenfords Post Office, Selkirk. Formerly an inn, built sometime between 1755-1772, when the highway between Torwoodlee and the Tweed was built. The left hand two bays, now the post office with a bedroom above, was originally a stable and loft. The three bays to the right are now a house. The walls are harled.

Handsome stable block, built 1791, at Hallyards, three miles south west of Peebles.

Characteristic two storey stone-built house at Crail, Fife, with living quarters on the first floor, and storage below. Access from the street is via a forestair.

Small farmhouse, built 1804 at Carlops, originally an inn. Its simple symmetrical facade and plain gabled parapets are characteristic of the smaller houses of the period.

Three bay cottage near Kelso, Roxburghshire.

district of Berwickshire, was prepared to support the establishment of a brick-and-tile works. One of the most notable of the village improvement schemes, and also one of the earliest, was Ormiston in East Lothian. It was begun in 1734 by the local laird, the agricultural reformer John Cockburn. It was designed as the market centre for his estates as well as a thriving focus for rural industry in the locality. A brewery and distillery were founded and textile manufacture established.

Most of the settlements continued the old traditions, using local materials and the well-tried methods of detail. The two-storey symmetrically-planned house, modelled on the parish manse or smaller houses of the 18th century, became standard, but the detached dwelling was too expensive to build and so the semi-detached house or long row or terrace of houses was developed. But some of the earliest improved cottages were a product of the period at the beginning of the Industrial Revolution. At Torbex, in Stirling District in Central Region, there are some fine 18th century weavers' houses while the weaving village of Carlops, in Tweeddale in Borders Region, was founded by the local laird in 1784. The cottages, built in a row, consisted of a kitchen combined with a workshop but separated from a parlour by a through passage. The partition walls, known as Galashiels partition, were constructed of panels of stone chippings set within strong timber frames. Most of these workers' houses were typical of the small, semi-industrial communities. At Chartershall, in

Stirling, the nailmakers' houses of the late 18th century have a central entrance with a living room on either side. At the end of each house is a workshop with its own separate entrance.

The little burgh of Gatehouse-of-Fleet once boasted a brewery, tannery, cotton mills, a boat-building yard and a bobbin factory. In the 18th century the laird canalized the River Fleet and the port of Gatehouse began to flourish, but during the following century industry began to recede from the Galloway towns. However, seams of coal and iron ore in Strathclyde Region were being worked. In this region the finer houses were made of granite while the small houses and cottages were built of whinstone, a hard sandstone, quarried from the lowland belt of grey-brown shale running right across Dumfries and Galloway.

The characterisic border country of Roxburgh, Selkirk and Peebles in the south east Lowlands was almost unaffected by the Industrial Revolution since they had neither iron nor coal to export. But the border hills had long provided sheep runs and the weaving of tweeds was already an established tradition. Here, as in the north of England, the industry moved from the domestic economy of weavers working in their own cottages to the large-scale mills in Hawick, Galashiels, Walkerburn and Innerleithen.

While Central and West Fife concentrated on agriculture and coal mining during most of the Industrial Revolution, nearly half the population of Scotland was centred in the Lowlands in and around the

Nos. 63-67 High Street, Peebles. Harled building with central gablet crowned by a chimney.

Kilbucho Place, Peeblesshire. Built originally as a rectangular two storey block in the mid 17th century, a large north wing was added in the early 18th century.

Old Manse, Kilbucho, Peeblesshire, mid 18th century, now used as a farmhouse. To the rear is a semi-circular staircase tower.

18th century cottages, Roxburgh Village, Roxburghshire.

157

The Old Post Office, Roxburgh Village, Roxburghshire.

Late 18th century houses, Causewayend, Ancrum, Roxburgh. The walls are harled and the roofs covered in slate, although one was originally thatched.

County Hotel, Peebles, 18th century. The central gablet is missing its chimney.

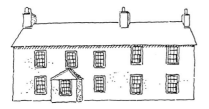

18th century tacksman's house, Ardlarach, Luing.

Synton House, Selkirk. Originally a single 3 storey high building built c.1777. Large extensions were added to both sides of the main block in the 19th century.

great Victorian city of Glasgow. The general adoption of coke fuel for smelting iron ore instead of charcoal during the latter part of the 18th century led to the large-scale establishment of the industry in the Central Lowlands where ironstone and coal were in abundance. The Carron Ironworks, established at Carron, in Stirling District in Central Region, in 1759 was planned to be the major iron-producing company in Britain. In 1779 a small coke furnace was built at Wilsontown, in the old county of Lanarkshire, now in Strathclyde Region, while the Carron Company developed the nail trade at Cromond, Midlothian.

They built industrial housing for the workers in the iron mills. During the same year the first effective cotton mill was established at Rothesay. Within a decade over twenty mills were in operation. The most important cotton-spinning centre was at New Lanark, in Strathclyde, founded by David Dale and Richard Arkwright in 1783. The manufacturing village they established was an experiment in community living controlled and managed by Dale's son-in-law, Robert Owen. Under Owen's far-sighted social experiments the Scots quickly became willing members of a community very foreign to their own.

Roads in the lowlands were improved, canals built and, by the turn of the 19th century with the introduction of new machinery, the wool trade, originally a domestic industry like the linen trade, became firmly established in the mills of Galashiels and Selkirk. Workers from Ireland and evicted crofters from the Highlands flocked to the new industries.

The Scottish Highlands & Islands

The character of most Highland houses was formed by the fierce Atlantic winds and storms that each building was designed to keep out. For obvious reasons little was imported. Before 1800 most of the rural labourers and artisans in the forested districts of Inverness, in the Highland Region, lived in some form of primitive timber-framed building. In the treeless outer islands, before the era of the lighthouse, the numerous ships wrecked along the coast cast ashore an ample supply of timber for the roof timbers of houses. Many houses in Tiree have such roof timbers.

The typical form of construction was the use of crucks, or couples, as they are known in Scotland. Most crucks were single blades of timber, but in Skye and the western Highlands many couples are jointed at wall-head level, the lower blade being scarfed and pegged to the upper one. Numerous examples of cruck-framed buildings survive in the central and western Highlands and in southwest Scotland. Up to the end of the 18th century many of these buildings were walled with wattle and turf while roofs were covered with branches and turf and then thatched.

Genuine black houses are found today only in the outer Isles, but in Skye there is a variation of the typical black houses of the Hebrides. Here the characteristic detail is the hip-ended roof and the overhanging eaves of thatch. The older plans included house and byre under one roof. The fire was in an open hearth with a small smoke vent above. One end of the black house was always higher than the other. The byre was at the lower end. In the earlier days there was no partition between the byre where the cattle were kept and the living room, and men

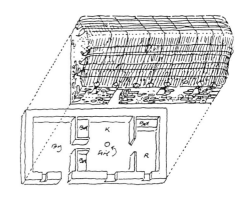

The Dalriadic type of black house has more conspicuous windows. The stone walls are usually about two feet or more in thickness, the stones roughly dressed to provide square corners, jambs and lintels. A characteristic feature is the use of box beds to form a partition between lobby and kitchen; the door of the kitchen was placed between the end of the box beds.

Early 19th century terrace, Hopeman, Morayshire.

159

Milton, Ross and Cromarty.
One of a number of planned 18th century villages. Of interest here is the informal, but ordered, grouping of terraces.

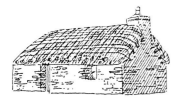

Dalriadic type of black house, Isle of Mull.

Dalriadic type of black house, Skye.

Chimneys were added later to the black houses, either at one or both gable ends.

attempted to shut out the cows from a veiw of the fire. A partition was eventually erected and then, later still, the byre was built as a separate building. The revised house plan then consisted of an entry door centred in the long wall. At one end would be the kitchen, at the other a large room, and the two were divided by an entry hall and a closet, large enough to accommodate a bed. A fireplace was usually built into each end wall, the short chimney just protruding above the ridge. In some houses the fireplace and chimney were placed on the internal cross wall. A distinctive characteristic is the way in which the thatch is dressed and bound around the protruding chimney. In some houses the hanging chimney is more common; here the flue was made of a wood box. It was enlarged to make a hood over the hearth and the whole chimney was fixed to the wall.

Where more space was needed, rooms were added on the kitchen end. Sometimes a storm porch would be built to cover the entrance from draughts. The walls were built of undressed stone. Most corners were rounded, but where dressed stone was available the corners were square. Most roof trusses were of the collar-beam type, while branches with a bed of turf and thatch formed the roof cover, the eaves extending over the external wall. The thatch was roped and weighted by stones tied just above the eaves or hanging down the face of the wall. Later ropes were replaced by wire netting. The stones were suspended from the wire netting by hoops of wire. Windows set deep in the wall were usually arranged symmetrically on either side of the entrance door. Floors were normally of beaten earth, but some cottages had wooden floors. Most rooms were open to the roof rafters, but later ceilings were installed. Internal walls were whitewashed or lined with wood boarding and covered with paper.

Another variation of the black house, found in the former county of Argyll now in Strathclyde, and West Perth and Kinross in Tayside Region, differs little in plan but is distinguished by end walls carried up to the ridge of the roof to form a gable. But, like the black houses of Skye, the thatch is carried over the front edge of the house to form overhanging eaves. Roof pitches were fairly steep, and fireplaces and chimneys were built on to the end walls.

Windows were characterized by large lintels. Some houses had ceilings and lofts. The cross wall in the kitchen was usually formed by a double bed box, with a central entry hall and closet and a further room beyond. This gable-ended cottage was universally popular and is found in most parts of the Highlands.

Places affect people and people affect places. It is difficult to say how much of the highly distinctive character of the Highlander was shaped and moulded by the bleak mountains and isolated glens of the remote northwest. One can clearly see, however, how the Celts themselves adapted to their environment. They did not tend to build towns or cities but lived in extended communities or clans held together by family ties and by loyalty to their chiefs, to whom indeed most of them were highly conscious of being related, however remotely. So closely knit were the communities of these mountain refuges and offshore islands that, until the present century, they preserved an older way of life that had long since disappeared from the more accessible Lowlands. They lived by cattle droving, by following their chiefs in war and by hunting. Agriculture and fisheries were not

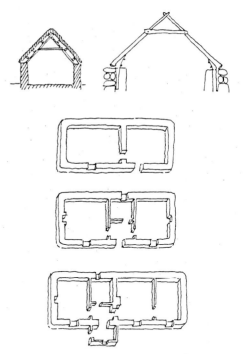

The Skye type of black house usually consists of two rooms, byre and house open to the roof. The fire was originally open hearth. Chimneys and fireplaces were added later. Windows were few and small. The byre was later converted into a living room, the animals being housed in an attached byre. A Draught lobby was built onto some houses in the 19th century.

One-and-a-half storey type housing in the planned village of Rothes, Grampian Region, built 1766. Note the characteristic stone gabled dormers of this type of terrace housing.

18th century three bay stone-built house, Argyllshire.

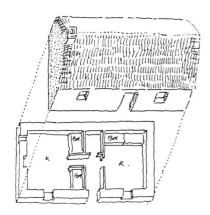

Prototype for the characteristic Highland cottage.

Row of four weavers' cottages, Jericho.

Below: Late 18th and early 19th century houses linked by a chapel, Kilcheran, Lismore. The domestic epitome of Ruskin's notion of changefulness, in which the occasional projection (providing the programme required it) was seen as a welcome addition to the interestingness of a compositional group.

highly cultivated, while crofting and sea fishing, which still sustain those who live in the remoter parts today, are more recent developments.

Cattle rearing dominated the Highland economy in the early 17th century. Until the mid-19th century great herds of cattle were driven annually to the markets of the Scottish Lowlands. During the more stable times preceding the Jacobite Rebellion, the population, freed from smallpox following the developments in vaccination by Edward Jenner in 1798, increased rapidly. The division of crofts resulted in more and more people occupying smaller holdings.

The stone used to build the traditional black houses was not always readily available. Clay had been used as a filler for slate and wattle walls and for wattle chimney hoods, but in 17th century Aberdeenshire, now part of Grampian Region, mud walling was used not only for building the humble cottages but for the building of manses, churches and town houses. Clay was mixed with straw and the walls built up like the cob cottages of Devon. But at the vulnerable points, such as the sides of doors and windows and the corners of houses,

Ballachulish House, Northern Strathclyde. Built of harled rubble with a slate roof, it has an L-shaped plan; the original house, built c.1764, is to the left. The west wing, to the right, was added in 1799.

House, Balliveolan, built c.1768. The original house was the three bays to the right. Built of harled rubble, it is an example of the typical, small laird's house of the late 18th century.

Manse, Dalmally. Designed by a local architect in 1804-5. Curious central gablet with chimney below which is a venetian window. The projecting entrance porch is flanked by two more venetian windows.

Dunollie House, built 1746 with further extension in the early 19th century - has all the simplicity and directness that W.R. Lethaby admired in the vernacular tradition.

hewn stone was used where possible. The walls were built in courses of varying depth and thickness. Where the roof was supported by cruck trusses or a framed structure, the walls were non-loadbearing and less substantial, but where loads had to be carried then the courses were made lower and thicker. The walls were usually built on stone or cobble footings which acted as a kind of damp-proof course.

In Moray most clay buildings were confined to towns but in the countryside of Nairn, Banff and Buchan and Gordon the better houses were made of stone while the humbler dwellings were of turf daubed

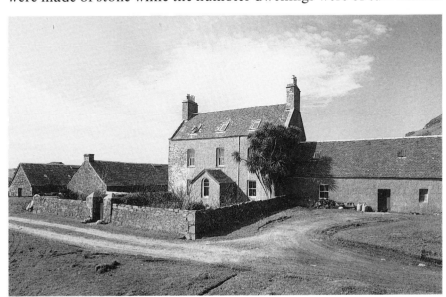

Farmhouse and farm buildings, Degnish, Argyllshire.

163

There are some good vernacular buildings in Stonehaven. 19th century Stonehaven is above the harbour. Old Stonehaven is wrapped around the harbour.

18th century labourer's cottage, Tayinloan, Argyllshire.

with clay plaster or alternating layers of turf and stone. In parts of Moray, and Banff and Buchan clay was mixed with sand and straw. This mixture, combined with large stones, was used in the construction of many houses built in the towns of Banff, Aberdeen and Turriff in the late 19th century. The first houses of the clay city in Luthermuir, in Kincardine and Deeside, in the Grampian Region, were built by squatters from the clay beneath their feet. They were begun in the late 18th century and by the mid-19th century were occupied mainly by handloom weavers. In parts of the old county of Perthshire, now in Tayside Region, most buildings were built of clay while in the north east of Scotland, particularly between Fife and Moray, clay thatching was a particular feature at this time. The thatch was laid in a vertical course from eaves to ridge and then clayed over before the second course was laid into position.

Many of the houses of the east coast towns exhibit the roll-moulded surrounds, crow-stepped gables and angle turrets typical of the 17th century. Walls were often built of granite while roofs were usually stone slates. Some mid-18th century houses were built of blocks of peat, stone and broom, and some town houses had their street facades especially stuccoed or rubble faced. Arbroath, a prosperous manufacturing centre of the late 18th century, has some attractive colour washed houses with the characteristic forestairs.

A primitive form of iron smelting had been carried on in many parts of Scotland since early times, but it was the establishment of the Invergarry furnace in 1727 that brought the Industrial Revolution to

Late 18th century house, Achlian, Argyllshire.

Porch detail of house at Achlian.

the Highlands. Wood for furnace charcoal was almost impossible to obtain but the Highlands had plenty, so ore was shipped from the Lancashire and Cumbrian mines. The smelted pig iron was returned southwards.

The linen trade was essentially domestic until well into the 19th century, but with the introduction of machine spinning, it established itself firmly in Fife, Perth and Kinross, and Angus.

By the late 18th century the cotton industry was firmly established in Perth and Kinross District at the Stanley Cotton Mills. Housing was scarce, and a model industrial village of two-storeyed houses of stone and brick was built in 1785. But by the second half of the 18th century many Scottish landowners had become convinced of the need to found village communities, partly to stimulate trade and partly to resettle the rural population displaced by the changing agrarian economy. Fochabers, in the District of Moray in Grampian Region, was a replanned village of whitewashed housing built round a larger market square in the late 18th century. It was built by the 4th Duke of Gordon and replaced an earlier village which had been removed when the castle was extended. The industrial housing of Deanston Park in Perthshire, Central, was built in the late 18th century for Buchanan and Arkwright. The houses were again whitewashed giving a clean and cheerful aspect, and each was provided with a garden.

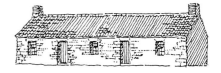

Random rubble walled cottages, with pantiled roof, Doune, Perth, Tayside Region.

165

Twin combination, Lewis.

(a)

Triple combination, Lewis.

View externally (a) and section through (b) a characteristic triple combination black house on Lewis.

(b)

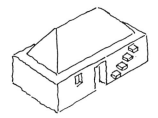

Axonometric of the Hebridean type of black house. The characteristic feature is the exposed broad ledge of wall top which extends around the house.

Northern Scotland

Of all the Highland areas of Scotland, the island of Lewis is the last to retain the seasonal migration of herds from a winter settlement to summer pastures. The practice, which allowed the grazing lands of the winter settlement to recover while giving cattle the benefit of the fresh hill pastures, was once widespread throughout the highland areas of Europe.

On the mainland the herdsmen built shielings for shelter on the summer pastures. Frequently constructed of turf and wattle, here, in the Western Isles, they were built of a dry-stone wall of boulders. The walls, usually about five feet in thickness, consisted of two layers of stone with an infilling of earth. The roof was covered in turf. The basic plans differed little from the shielings of Cumbria, but the older shielings, used until the beginning of the 19th century, were generally circular in plan with a dome-shaped roof of corbelled stone. This technique of construction recalls the early Christian oratories of Scotland and Ireland. In some instances these beehive shielings, as they are referred to in this area, were grouped together to form a complex of linked apartments. The construction of the corbelled-stone roof limited the size of shielings to less than fourteen feet. As larger rooms were required the rectangular plan with a timber roof became common.

The winter settlements were much more substantial affairs, but here again, the nature of materials available, the harshness of the climate and the general economy of the land largely fashioned the crofts in the

Crofter's cottage, Dunganachy, Benbecula.

166

austere and utilitarian manner seen today. The croft is a tiny farm, often less than five acres in size. Here the crofter and his family could earn a bare but basic living, supplemented by fishing, weaving or possibly building roads in the area.

The numerous bays and inlets of Lewis and Harris made excellent harbours for small boats and ideal sites for tiny villages. Inshore fishing was good in a hinterland studded with trout lochs. But the lack of soil made it necessary for the crofters to make their own soil for tillage. In the hollows of the rocks, selected becaue of the good drainage, they built up platforms of peat. Across this platform they spread seaweed which they had carried up in creels from the shore. On these beds, or lazybeds as they are called, they planted potatoes and oats.

This is the traditional way of life in the Highlands and Islands. In Sutherland most of the inhabitants are crofters. Here the proportion of arable land is the lowest in Scotland, with much of the area given over to sheep runs and deer forests. It was here that the Norsemen were dominant between the 11th and 13th centuries.

Caithness offers more promise to the farmer than Sutherland despite the wide tracts of moorland suitable only for game or for grazing. Fishing, the second main industry, provides the necessary supplementary income. The richest arable land is found in Orkney and

Three bay croft, Laide, Sutherland.

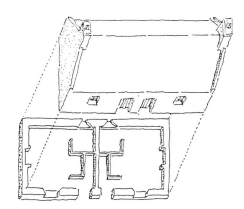

Typical plan and form of the *improved* cottage of the early to mid 19th century. Note the fireplace built into each gable end. Black houses were still quite common in the early 19th century. Gradually they were replaced by the improved *white* cottages like this, either single cell or double cell.

167

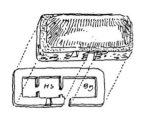

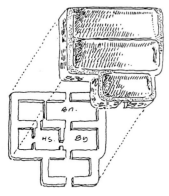

Most of the Hebridean black houses are planned as a long oblong divided into three rooms. The entrance door led directly through the brye to the house. Many houses on the Isle of Lewis were planned with two or three buildings joined along their side. These are the most primitive form of black house. By the end of the 18th century, the central, open hearth of such houses was being replaced by a fireplace in the gable end of the house.

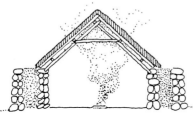

Section through a black house of the Hebrides. The walls are generally very thick, varying from four to eight feet, and built of stone facings, inside and out, the central core being filled with stones, gravel or earth. The corners of the buildings are rounded. The roof is set on the inside of the walls. The rainwater discharged from the roof is caught in the central core, or hearting, and from there percolates to the ground making a damp blanket of earth which prevents the strong winds penetrating through the dry-stone wall.

Lerwick, Shetlands. A picturesque harbour of 18th and 19th century warehouses and terraces.

the Orcadians are famous farmers; they are a self-contained and prosperous people. Whereas the Shetlander is said to be a sailor and fisherman who has a small croft, the Orcadian is said to be a farmer who has a boat.

In this comparatively spartan area the local building tradition has been retained and much of its original character can be seen. The greatest changes occurred during the notorious Highland clearances, sparked off by the Jacobite Rebellion of 1745. In an attempt to smoke out this rebellious area the government did its best to destroy the Highland tradition. The Highlanders were disarmed, their national dress prohibited and Gaelic made a shameful tongue. Whichever side the Highlander had taken he was made to feel inferior to the English. This was followed by the anit-Gael, anti-Celt policy of the Highland clearances. There were various reasons for the tragedy, many originating in events before the '45, but it was the '45 that accelerated the disaster. Many Highlanders, seeing greater profits in sheep farming, began to evict their clansmen. Later the moorlands and mountainsides were turned into great sporting grounds. These clearances lasted until the late 19th century when a series of Crofters Acts were passed protecting the rights of the Highland peasant.

Typical burgh houses of the late 16th and 17th centuries are to be found at Kirkwall in Orkney. Most are built of local flagstone laid in clay mortar and roofed with heavy stone slates. The house fronts are narrow and they are also usually gabled. Cromarty Harbour which had been destroyed by the sea was rebuilt in the late 18th century by the local laird, George Ross, to serve his newly-established hempencloth factory. This sudden prosperity is reflected in the more spacious two- and three-storey town houses. The fairly plain houses built of red sandstone rubble are occasionally characterized by rusticated quoins and the provision of a radial fanlight over the entrance doors.

By the early 19th century there was a considerable amount of building. The Marquess of Stafford built two ports in Sutherland. One, Brora, now a holiday centre, was built between 1811 and 1813 as a coal-mining and salt-producing centre. The other was Helmsdale, a herring and fishing port founded in 1814. Each was laid out on a

regular grid plan. The Marquess of Stafford, one of the largest landowners in the Highlands, had been severely criticized for his behaviour during the clearances. The two ports were, if anything, a belated attempt to exonerate himself. Skilled craftsmen were introduced to teach new trades; bricks and tiles were manufactured on the estate for the vast building programme, while the improved house designs began revolutionizing standards of rural and urban housing in this part of Scotland.

Standard layouts were developed and financial inducements were offered to workers for the most soundly-built dwellings. Numerous ideas were developed in pattern books concerning improved cottages for the labouring classes. Many of these trim one-storey cottages proposed were built on numerous estate villages.

Chimneys and wider windows were added to many traditional Skye types of black house.

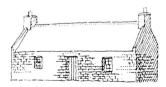

Archetypal crofter's cottage, Clachtoll, Sutherland. This is one of the so-called *white* houses built to replace the black houses of the early 19th century.

Ireland

From the Middle Ages until the mid-19th century one of the main characteristics of the predominantly pastoral economy of Ireland was the summer migration of herdsmen and their families to the lusher pastures in the mountains as was the tradition in the rest of Europe. Similar to many nomadic herdsmen, they travelled considerable distances from their winter settlements and needed to build some kind of rudimentary shelter; these were known as booleys and they are not unlike the shielings of Northumberland and Cumbria.

They were usually built of sods on a foundation of earth and stone. Some were built of stone when it was available as in Achill Island, County Mayo. They consisted of one large room, either oval in plan or rectangular with rounded corners. They varied in size, the average room being about 10 feet by 20 feet. In the bogland areas, they were built into a sloping bank of peat or gravel. The roofs were constructed of bog timbers and covered by long strips of sod and thatched with heather secured by ropes. There were no windows and usually only one door opening positioned in one of the long walls. Occasionally a second door would be made in the long wall opposite. The fire was placed in an open hearth along one of the walls.

Their winter home, the bally, was a slightly more substantial dwelling built of clay or loose stones with green sods as a filler for the gaps. Shelter from the prevailing winds was essential, the result being groups of between twenty and sixty houses arranged in a disorderly cluster. This small settlement, usually called a clachan, had none of the features of the traditional village such as a church, inn or shops. The houses were small, usually one storey in height, rectangular in plan and never more than one room in width.

A characteristic feature in the north and west was the presence of a

Kibline Castle, Tullaherin, Co. Kilkenny. One of the fascinating aspects of both townscape and landscape in Ireland is the juxtaposition of different scaled volumes. The country gentry in the 18th century began to add more comfortable houses to such towers. The bawn became a garden.

Dwyer-MacAllister Cottage, Derrynamuck, Co. Wicklow. Two-roomed, thatch-roofed, 18th century cottage, once the house of the famous rebel, Michael Dwyer, leader of the Wicklow uprising of 1798.

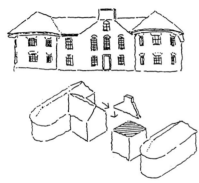

Assolas, Castlemegner, Co. Cork. Intriguing combination of volumes - truncated 17th century tower house capped by a gable crowned with a chimney and flanked asymmtrically by bow-fronted wings.

Ardress House, Co. Armagh. The house was remodelled by George Ensor in the 1770s with the addition of two false bays at each end to complete the alignment with the garden.

(a) Two house-shops, Askeaton, Co. Limerick. Of interest in the smaller towns are the so-called front-parlour shops- a strategy the new towns might well have considered experimenting with.

Westport, Co. Mayo. Gracious Georgian town and former port, surrounded by trees and mountains on the edge of Clew Bay. It is a planned town designed by James Wyatt in 1780. Fine 18th century terraces align the granite walled quayside along the River Carrowbeg.

front and a back door, each one opposite the other. This was possibly a means of regulating the draught from the open fire, much like the positioning of windows in the medieval Welsh hall house. When the chimney flues were added the back door was often blocked up or turned into a window or cupboard. Where a byre was under the same roof, then the second door was retained and the passage served as a path for livestock as well. In many rural areas this was the traditional type of dwelling. Many had rounded ends and hipped roofs. Later the gabled house was typical in most of western Ireland. Fires were burned in the traditional central hearth which acted as a room divider. Some of the more substantial houses had at least three rooms. At Menlough, in north east Galway, the house walls, built of local limestone, are two to three feet thick. Roofs are thatched with sedge from the nearby lake. The open-field form of farming predominated in these areas, although a few people specialized in weaving and thatching.

The basic form of the traditional Irish house differs little. Most, particularly in the rural areas, consisted of a series of rooms each opening into the next, while roofs, determined by a predominantly rainy climate and also the nature of straw and reed which is used as a roof covering, are steeply pitched. The major differences occur in shape and detail, the most important influences being the availability of materials and building expertise which, in their turn, were governed largely by political, social and economic constraints.

There are three basic types of houses. One, rectangular in shape, consisted of a central open hearth which when a protecting wall was

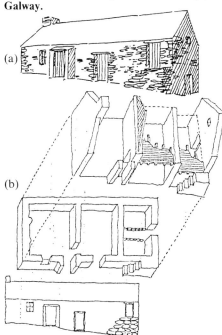

(a)

(b)

built around one side of the hearth, divided the houses into two compartments – a living-kitchen room and a bedroom. In the second type the hearth was moved to the end wall. Control of draughts was necessary and a back and front door were built opposite each other. There was still a living-kitchen room, while the bedroom was formed behind a partition of heavy furniture consisting of a dresser or cupboard. The third type, found chiefly in the north east, has a fireplace at each end. The introduction of chimney flues meant that double doors could be dispensed with. The one door opened into the living-kitchen room. The bedroom was to one side behind a solid wall. In a corner of the main room in many parts of Ireland a bed boxed in with timber framing was common. In parts of Ulster and north west Connaught a typical feature was the bed built in a recess projecting out from the house. In this same region the byre, included under the same roof, formed the traditional longhouse. The back and front doors were usually retained. The cow entered by the front door but after making it was led out through the back door while another was brought in at the front. In some parts of north west Ulster, particularly along the Atlantic seaboard of County Donegal, many houses with byres were built down a steep slope. The upper or hearth end was built into the bank while the lower end, with side walls over twelve feet high, could be lofted over. Cattle were housed in the byre on the ground floor with a bedroom built above it. The bedroom and kitchen were on split levels. Where the cross passage in the traditional longhouse would have been, a ladder or stone steps were built to reach the bedroom. Both kitchen and bedroom were open to the roof rafters.

(a, b) Desmond McCourt has made a fascinating study of the custom, typical throughout Western Europe, of sharing the rural dwelling with livestock. In Ireland the tradition belongs to the longhouse type. Built against a slope or steep bank the byre is planned at the lower end thus giving enough headroom for inserting a loft in the roof space above. This example is near Glenelly, Co. Tyrone.

(c)

(c) The loft space was used either as a bedroom, reached from within the house, or as additional storage space, reached by steps from outside, as in this example near Burtonport, Co. Donegal.

(d)

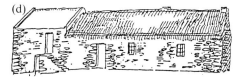

(d) House near Baribeg, Co. Donegal.

171

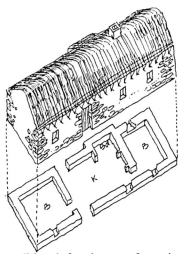

The traditional farmhouse of south-west Donegal has a long rectangular plan with a cross passage between the byre and domestic quarters. A characteristic feature is the bed alcove beside the kitchen hearth.

Circular pavilion, Belline, Co. Kilkenny. One of two detached three-storey high circular pavilions each with a central chimney. The childless owners entertained in the main house whilst each occupied a pavilion in the grounds. The eccentric client was Peter Walsh, born in 1740.

Parliament Street, Kilkenny, Co. Kilkenny. Handsome double doorway articulated by Tuscan columns with an elliptical fanlight above.

Four bay thatch-roofed cottage, Co. Galway.

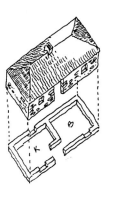 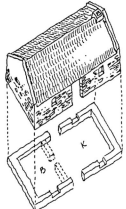 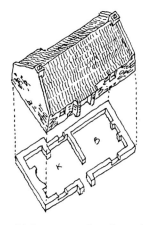

Left: The traditional dwelling of rural Ireland is a one storey high, rectangular planned thatch-roofed house no more than one room in width. Of this traditional type there seem to be three basic variants, as Caoimhin O Danachair has pointed out. This two roomed house with hipped roof is characteristic of eastern and south-eastern Ireland.

Centre: The second type is found in West Ulster, Connaught and West Munster. It has two entrances ranged opposite each other, gable ends, a single fireplace with the bedroom partially closed off by a light timber partition or large piece of furniture.

Right: The third type is characteristic of both north-eastern Ireland as well as Scotland. It is a two roomed house with a chimney planned at both gable ends. Note the typical bed alcove here built in an outshut beside the kitchen hearth.

Dry-stone walling was used to build houses in many parts of Ireland. This was a fairly traditional form of building dating back to the early Christian clochain and oratories, but the best material of all

for those who could afford it was mortar and stone. Lintels to doors and windows were usually made of timber but where large stones were available they were used for lintels.

Roofs were steeply pitched. In East Ulster roof rafters were carried on large purlins which span between the gable walls and cross walls, but elsewhere the lighter coupled rafters with a collar were more common. Most were covered with strips of sod laid straight onto the roof timbers. The finish was usually a thatch of straw or heather. In County Down straw was laid in specially prepared bundles and the thatch plastered down at the eaves, gable and ridge with clay or mud. Along the Atlantic coast the thatch was secured by ropes tied to stone weights or, as along the Antrim coast, with ropes pegged to the wall tops. But over most of the country, thatch was secured by twigs to the sod beneath.

Many houses, particularly in North Antrim in the late 18th century, were adapted to meet the changing economy as domestic linen manufacture began to replace small-scale farming. A typical feature of the old weavers' cottages is the outshut built to take a loom. By the late 18th century the weaving industry expanded and in some cases a separate loom shop was added forming a three-bay, or in south west Lough Neagh, a four-bay house. But by the late 19th century domestic linen manufacture began to decline.

Larger two-storey houses were generally rebuilt along more fashionable lines or remodelled during the 18th century. Thatch was

Typical village houses, Finuge, Co. Limerick.

Bonnetstown, St Canice, Co. Kilkenny. Built in 1737 for a client unable to afford the services of one of the more talented architects of the time. A local builder was employed instead to make a variant on the architectural ideas then currently fashionable. Beautiful window surrounds along the piáno nobile.

173

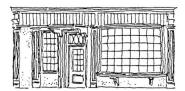

Shop front, Kilkenny. Bow-fronted Georgian style shop front and canopied entrance framed by fluted pilasters.

Bearforest, Mallow, Co. Cork. Grand but unostentatious villa style house with boldy curved portico designed 1807-08 by Sir Richard Morrison.

A characteristic feature of many Irish towns in the late 18th and early 19th centuries were handsome town house, generally regular and plain, usually of brick, but always enriched by a handsome entrance.

Rustic lodge, Belline, Co. Kilkenny. Laugier's archetypal temple here built as a gate lodge with tree truck columns and capitals of whitewashed rope. It was built in the ground of Peter Walsh's house at Belline.

replaced by slate, a trend which continued into the early twentieth century, but for the humbler dwellings such changes occur mainly in this century when thatch has given way to corrugated iron or the asbestos tile.

The poverty of accommodation and general misery of the labouring poor was due, among other things, to exploitation, indifference and mismanagement. Some 18th and 19th century landlords did replan their tenants' housing. Some created whole villages, usually aping some distant Utopia. Bagenalstown (Muine Bheag in County Carlow) was to have been called Versailles, while another, Moy, in County Tyrone, was built around a long narrow square and laid out on the plan of Marengo in Lombardy. But most adopted the traditional materials and house plans of the area.

Restoring the Georgian House

An interesting aspect of post-war Britain has been the unparalleled growth of amenity societies. However, the earliest of such societies was formed over a century ago when 27 citizens formed the Sidmouth Improvement Committee, " . . . for the purpose of proposing plans for the improvement of the place . . . and also for securing to the public the existing walks on the cliffs and Salcombe Hill . . ." Two decades later the Commons, Open Spaces and Footpaths Preservation Society was formed in 1865 by John Stuart Mill, T. H. Huxley, Octavia Hill and Robert Hunter. among others, as an article in Official Architecture and Planning of September 1968 reported, " . . . to fight enclosures of land resulting from the outward spread of London and the growing demand for land for rebuilding". The preservations of open spaces such as Hampstead Heath, Plumstead Common and Wandsworth Common are due to this Society. But by far the most prestigious and influential of these 19th century Societies was that of the Society for the Protection of Ancient Buildings. SPAB, as it is generally known, was founded by William Morris in 1877. The idea for the Society sprang from a proposal made by John Ruskin in 1854 that, " . . . watchers and agents throughout the country should report on the state of old buildings and monuments so that steps might be taken to preserve them". Eighteen years later, in 1895, the National Trust, soon to become one of the largest landowners in the country, was founded by Octavia Hill, Robert Hunter and Canon Rawnsley.

Numerous other watchdog committees were formed during the early twentieth century. The Ancient Monuments Society was founded in 1924, " . . . for the study and conservation of ancient monuments, historic buildings and fine old craftsmanship". Two years later, in 1926, the Council for the Preservation of Rural England was formed. The Georgian Group, born out of the passion and anger felt by people such as Lord Derwent, Douglas Goldring and Robert Byron at the wanton destruction of London's Architectural Heritage, was founded in 1937 to " . . . save Georgian buildings, monuments parks and gardens from destruction or disfigurement". In 1955 the Civic Trust was founded with the objective, amongst many, of " . . . stimulating the public interest in the good appearance of town and country and fostering, generally, a sense of civic pride".

All these Societies, included with addresses in a list at the back, provide general or technical advice and arrange lectures, as with the Georgian Group. SPAB, for instance, will advise on all problems affecting old buildings, giving technical advice on their treatment and repair. It also arranges annual courses on the repair of ancient buildings for architects, surveyors and builders, administers scholarships, circulates a quarterly list of buildings for sale in need of repairs, publishes a quarterly newspaper as well as a series of technical pamphlets. The well illustrated technical pamphlets are of particular interest, dealing as they do with such subjects as strengthening timber floors; treatment of damp in old buildings; cleaning stone and brick; pointing stone and brick walling; the care and repair of thatched roofs; chimneys in old buildings and fire safety in historic buildings. The pamphlet, Chimneys in Old Buildings, for instance gives a general introduction to domestic heating and then discusses the most common problems associated with chimneys, such as the deterioration of the structure by erosion of the mortar by the action of wind, rain or frost; fracturing of the brick or stone caused by settlement, unequal loading or frost; ingress of damp; smoking chimneys; the fire risk created by timber joists and beams buried in the flue walls or even exposed on the internal face of the flue; the accumulation of pockets of soot creating latent fire risk, simply because bends in the flue had prevented adequate sweeping. At the time of writing, each pamphlet cost £1.

In a marvellous book, *Repair of Ancient Buildings,* first published by J.M.Dent & Sons Ltd. in 1929 and since reprinted by SPAB in 1981, A.R.Powys, Secretary of the Society from 1911-1926, stated that the building repair was a "...highly specialised branch of Architecture". He felt that "...the questions which have to be dealt with are of a most intricate nature, always involving the consideration of the twin needs of structural stability and of conservation, and sometimes also of making alterations. In the course of work on an ancient building points difficult to decide and needing instant decisions constantly arise. What needs renewal? How much may be retained? What technical method should be employed? and like questions confront one at every turn". He felt that ancient fabric should be disturbed as little as possible, but where repairs were necessary they should be carried out with materials appropriate to the existing without recourse to ageing or staining.

The predeliction for fake fanlights as an integral part of neo-Georgian doors is a complete fantasy about the traditional Georgian, for in *real* Georgian architecture, the fanlight was generally a fan shaped glazed light crowning an opening. Georgian kitchens were often ill lit, labour intensive basement rooms, inconveniently positioned for modern day convenience unless great replanning is envisaged. How much replanning should one allow oneself? How authentic, in fact, should one's Georgian restoration be, after all absent from such homes were other modern conveniences, such as bathrooms. Even the proportional system employed was often less than strict. For the grander houses, the aesthetic rules were strictly adhered to, but for the small Georgian house or cottage the builder made do with a rough copy drawn, most likely, from the pages of one of Batty Langley's pattern books than from the more exact descriptions made by architects, fresh from the Grand Tour. Distorted these proportions may be, but they still have a charm and character that needs considerable care in restoration. Many Georgian builders were somewhat lackadaisical in the interpretation of classical models for few would have read Vitruvius. But despite such lapses, it would be unfortunate if less than meticulous care was taken today with what details they did incorporate.

We know many Tudor buildings were refaced in the Georgian period; we know casement windows of many 17th century houses were replaced by the more fashionable sliding sash windows of the 18th century. Should we now turn the clock back? And if we did, how far? They are not easy questions, as A.R.Powys pointed out. Everything depends on the particular context and scale of the proposed restoration. And the key is the dating of your house. As has been pointed out, you may well find a much earlier building behind the Georgian facade. The alterations to and restoration of your house should be appropriate to the original character of your house, preserving, where possible, and giving it renewed life. As A.R.Powys pointed out you should " . . . avoid making reproductions to take place of damaged features or missing parts when this involves the destruction and not the protection of what remains of the original work". SPAB, the Georgian Group and other societies, listed at the back, are happy to offer advice, both of a technical nature, as well as, in some cases, recommending suitably qualified specialists, including architects.

Apart from A. R. Powys' excellent book, *Repair of Ancient Buildings,* re-issued by SPAB in 1981, Hugh Lander's *The House Restorer's Guide,* published by David and Charles (1986), covers the problems of restoration of old houses in considerable detail from the availability of grants, the necessary planning permission and building approval, to the problem of damp walls and repairing sash windows, stairs and woodwork, flues and fireplaces.

In *Care for Old Houses,* published by Prisma Alpha (1984), Pamela Cunnington has an informative section dealing with the framework of conservation from the historical background and current legal position to financial aid at both central and local government level, including improvement grants (accommodating the provision of modern amenities); repair grants (for houses built before 1919 with basic amenities but needing structural repairs); special grants (offered for improvements as well as for providing means of escape in houses with multiple occupancy). This book, which is profusely illustrated, also discusses the problems of providing plumbing and sanitation, heating and insulation in old houses to modern standards. The use of softwood joinery and panelling in Georgian houses provided with central heating has caused serious shrinkage, hardly alleviated by humidifiers. Such conflicts created by the provision of modern comfort in Georgian houses are many. Resorting to 18th century costumes and candlelight would hardly be the answer either.

One of the most useful books, more a directory in fact, is *Putting Back the Style,* published by Evans Brothers Ltd (1982). There are excellent essays, including one on *The Georgian Terraced House* by Dan Cruickshank which discusses the inside and outside of the Georgian terraced house, how the house was used, the type of decorative detail, the use of plaster, colour etc. Indispensible are the chapters dealing with Architectural Metalwork, Flooring, Plasterwork, Woodwork, The Kitchen, Bathroom, Colour, Furniture, Lighting, Fabrics and Wallpaper, Architectural Salvage and Garden Furniture. Each section has a detailed list of suppliers' names, addresses and telephone numbers.

Whilst The Brooking Collection is a museum and information centre in White Lane, Guildford, covering architectural features from 1700 to 1935, the chances are that similar items could be purchased at either The London Architectural Salvage and Supply Co in Mark Street, London or at Walcot Reclamation in Walcot Street, Bath. In the directory is a supplier, Coles of Mortimer Street, London, with emulsion and oil colours not generally found on other lists; there is L. Cornelissen & Sons, a firm selling pure ground pigments suitable for use in distemper or for mixing with a white lead base, whilst Amazing Grates, of High Road, London N.2, has one of the largest stocks of Georgian, Victorian and Edwardian architectural fireplaces in London.

List of Useful Societies

Ancient Monuments Society

St Andrews by the Wardrobe, Queen Victoria Street, London EC4V 5DE

Founded in 1924. Concerned with the Study and Conservation of Ancient Monuments. Publisher an annual Study.

Building Conservation Trust

Apt 39, Hampton Court Palace, East Molesey, Surrey, KT8 9BS

Exhibition of proper repair and maintenance.

Civic Trust

17 Carlton House Terrace, London, SW1Y 5AW

Founded 1955. Concerned primarily with Townscape. Publishes numerous booklets and prepares exhibitions and films.

Crafts Council

12 Waterloo Place, London, SW1Y 4AV

Keeps register of conservation craftsmen and building suppliers on regional basis.

Georgian Group

2 Chester Street, London, SW1X 7BB

Originally a sub-committee of SPAB, it was founded in 1937. Provides advice on the conservation and restoration of Georgian property.

Historic Houses Association

38 Ebury Street, London SW1W 0LU

Provides advice and information for owners of historic houses.

Institute of Architectural Ironmongers

15 Soho Square, London, W1V 5FB

Paint Research Association

Waldegrave Road, Teddington, Middlesex, TW11 8LD

Landmark Trust

Shottesbrooke, Maidenhead, Berkshire.

Acquires and repairs smaller historic houses which it subsequently lets as holiday accommodation.

National Trust

36 Queen Anne's Gate, London, SW1H 9AS

Scottish Civic Trust

24 George Street, Glasgow, G2 1EF

National Trust for Scotland

5 Charlotte Street, Edinburgh, EH2 4DU

Scottish Georgian Group

39 Castle Street, Glasgow, G2 1EF

Society for the Protection of Ancient Buildings

37 Spital Square, London E1 6DY

Founded by William Morris in 1877, it organises courses and exhibitions, as well as providing technical advice on restoration and alterations to historic buildings.

Vernacular Architecture Group

Chy an Whyloron, Wigmore, Leominster, Hereford and Worcestershire, HR6 9UD

Bibliography

ADAMSON, G. *Machines in the Home.* Lutterworth, 1969.

ASLET, CLIVE and POWERS, ALAN. *The National Trust Book of the English House.* Viking, 1985.

ASHLEY, MAURICE. *England in the Seventeenth Century.* New edition, Hutchinson, 1978.

BARLEY, M.W. *The English Farmhouse and Cottage.* Routledge and Kegan Paul, 1972; *The House and Home.* Studio Vista, 1965; *Houses and History.* Faber and Faber, 1986.

BATSFORD, H. and FRY, C. *The English Cottage.* B.T. Batsford, 1938.

BAX, B. ANTHONY. *The English Parsonage.* John Murray, 1964.

BEARD, GEOFFREY. *The National Trust Book of English Furniture.* Viking, 1985.

BILLET, MICHAEL. *Thatched Buildings of Dorset.* Robert Hale, 1984.

BOUCH, C.M.L. and JONES, G.P. *The Lake Counties 1500-1830.* Manchester University Press, 1961.

BOWYER, J. *History of Building.* Crosby, Lockwood Staples, 1973.

BRAUN, HUGH. *Old English Houses.* Faber & Faber, 1962; *The Story of English Architecture.* Faber & Faber, 1954.

BROWN, A. *Colchester in the Eighteenth Century.* A.F.J. Brown, 172 Lexden Road, Colchester, Essex.

BRUNSKILL, R.W. *Illustrated Handbook of Vernacular Architecture.* Revised edition. Faber and Faber, 1978; *Vernacular Architecture of the Lake Counties.* New edition. Faber and Faber, 1978; *Houses.* Collins, 1982.

BURTON, ANTHONY. *Canal Builders.* Revised edition. David & Charles, 1981; *The Remains of a Revolution.* Andre Deutsch, 1975; he Canal Builders. Eyre Methuen, 1972.

BURTON, E. *The Georgians at Home.* Longman, 1967.

CAVE, LYNDON F. *The Smaller English House. Its History and Developement.* Hale, 1981.

CHALKIN, C.W. *The Provincial Towns of England.* Arnold, 1974.

CHAMBERS, JAMES. *The English House.* Methuen London Ltd, 1985.

CHAMBERS, J.D. and MINGAY, G.E. *The Agricultural Revolution 1750-1880.* B.T. Batsford, 1975.

CLIFTON-TAYLOR, ALEC. *The Pattern of English Building.* Faber and Faber, 1972.

COBBETT, WILLIAM. *Rural Rides.* Vols 1 & 2. J.M. Dent & Son, 1966.

COOK, OLIVE. *English Cottages and Farmhouses.* Thames and Hudson, 1982.

COSSONS, NEIL. *The B.P. Book of Industrial Architecture.* David and Charles, 1978.

CRUICKSHANK, D. *London: The Art of Georgian Building.* The Architectural Press, 1975; *A Guide to the Georgian Buildings of Britain and Ireland.* Weidenfeld and Nicolson, 1985.

CUNNINGTON, PAMELA. *Care for Old Houses.* Prism Alpha, 1984.

DANACHAIR, C.O. *Folk and Farms.* Royal Society of Antiquaries of Ireland, 1976.

DARLEY, GILLIAN. *Built in Britain: a view of traditional architecture.* Weidenfeld & Nicolson, 1983; *Villages of Vision.* The Architectural Press, 1975.

DEFOE, D. *Tour through the Island of Great Britain 1724-7.*

DOWNS, KERRY. *English Baroque Architecture.* D. Zwemmer Ltd, 1966.

DUNBAR, J.G. *The Historic Architecture of Scotland.* B.T. Batsford, 1966.

EDWARDS, RALPH. *Hepplewhite Furniture Design.* Alec Tiranti Ltd, 1965.

EVANS, TONY and LYCETT GREEN, CANDIDA. *English Cottages.* Weidenfeld and Nicolson, 1982.

FASTNEDGE, R. *English Furniture Styles.* Penguin, 1955.

FENTON, A. and WALKER, B. *The Rural Architecture of Scotland.* John Donald Publishers Ltd, 1981.

FIELD, H. and BUNNEY, M. *English Domestic Architecture in the Seventeenth and Eighteenth Centuries.* Bell, 1905.

FIENNES, C. Journals of the earliest years of the eighteenth century, edited by C. Morris as *The Journeys of Celia Fiennes.* Cresset Press, 1947.

FLETCHER, V. *Chimney Pots and Stacks.* Centaur, 1968.

FORRESTER, H. *The Smaller Queen Anne and Georgian House.* Tindal Press, 1964.

GAILEY, ALAN. *Rural Houses of the North of Ireland.* John Donald Publishers Ltd, 1984.

GARDINER, S. *Evolution of the House.* Constable, 1975.

GEORGE, M. DOROTHY. *England in Transition.* Penguin, 1953. *Hogarth to Cruickshank: Social Change in Graphic Satire.* Lane, 1967.

GIROUARD, MARK. *Life in the English Country House.* Yale, 1978.

GLOAG, JOHN. *English Furniture.* A & C Black Ltd, 1934.

GODFREY, W.H. *Our Building Inheritance.* Faber and Faber.

GORDON, S. *Highways and Byways in the West Highlands.* MacMillan London Ltd, 1979.

GUERNSEY SOCIETY, THE. *The Guernsey Farmhouse.* 1963.

HARRISON, B. and HUTTON, B. *Vernacular Houses in North Yorkshire and Cleveland.* John Donald Publishers Ltd, 1983.

HARVEY, J. *Sources of History of Houses.* British Records Association, 1974.

HARVEY, NIGEL. *A History of Farm Buildings in England and Wales.* David and Charles, 1984.

HELLYER, S.S. *Plumbing.* 1873.

HENDERSON, A. *The Family House in England.* Phoenix, 1964.

HOBHOUSE, H. *Thomas Cubitt, Master Builder.* MacMillan, 1971.

HMSO. *Rural Houses of West Yorkshire, 1400-1830.* 1986; *Rural Houses of the Lancashire Pennines, 1560-1760.* 1985; Inventories of the Ancient and Historical Monuments of: *Argyll Volume 1 - Kintyre.* 1971; *Argyll Volume 2 - Lorn.* 1975; *The County of Roxburgh* Volumes 1 and 2. 1956; *Selkirk.* 1957; *Stirlingshire* Volume 1. 1963.

HOLME, T. *Chelsea.* Hamish Hamilton, 1972.

HOSKINS, W.G. *The Making of the English Landscape.* Penguin, 1975; *English Landscapes.* BBC Publications.

HOWITT, W. *Rural Life in England.* 1838.

HUDSON, KENNETH. The Archaeology of Industry. The Bodley Head, 1976.

HUSSEY, C. *English Country Houses, 1715-1840* Volumes 1-3. Country Life, 1955-8.

HYAMS, EDWARD. *English Cottage Gardens.* Thomas Nelson & Sons, 1970.

INNOCENT, C.F. *Development of English Building Construction.* David and Charles, 1971.

JEKYLL, GERTRUDE. *Old English Household Life.* B.T. Batsford, 1925.

JOHNSON, S. *Journey to the Western isles of Scotland.* 1775.

JONES, S.R. *English Village Homes.* B.T. Batsford, 1936.

KELLY, A. *The Book of English Fireplaces.* Country Life, 1968.

KENT, N. *Hints to Gentlemen of Landed Property.* 1775.

LAING, D. *Hints for Dwellings.* 1801.

LANDER, HUGH. *The House Restorer's Guide.* David and Charles, 1986.

LANGLEY, BATTY. *The City and Country Workman's Treasury of Design.* 1741.

LOUDEN, J.C. *Encylopaedia of Cottage, Farm and Villa Architecture.* 1883.

LOWNDES, WILLIAM. *The Royal Crescent in Bath: A Fragment of English Life.* The Radcliffe Press, 1981.

LUCAS, Dr. *An Essay on Waters.* 1756.

LLOYD, N. *History of the English House.* Architectural Press, 1975.

MALTON, J. *Designs for Villas.* 1802.

MARSHALL, J.P. *Old Lakeland.* David and Charles, 1971.

MAYHEW, H. *London Labour and the London Poor.* 1851.

MERCER, ERIC. *English Vernacular Houses.* HMSO, 1975.

MOXON, J. *Mechanick Exercises.* 1678.

MUIR, RICHARD. *The English Village.* Thames and Hudson, 1980.

MUTHESIUS, STEFAN. *The English Terraced House.* Yale, 1982.

NAISMITH, ROBERT J. *Buildings of the Scottish Countryside.* Victor Gollancz Ltd, 1985.

OLIVER, BASIL. *The Cottages of England.* B.T. Bastford, 1929.

OSBORNE, A. *English Domestic Architecture.* Country Life, 1954.

PALMER, R. *The Water Closet.* David and Charles, 1973.

PALMER COOK, F. *Talk to Me of Windows.* Allen, 1971.

PAPWORTH, J. *Rural Residences.* 1818.

PENOYRE, JOHN and JANE. *Houses in the Landscape.* Faber and Faber, 1978.

PLAW, J. *Sketches for Country Houses, Villas and Rural Dwellings.* 1800.

PLUMB, J.H. *England in the Eighteenth Century.* Penguin, 1950.

POWYS, A.R. *Repair of Ancient Buildings.* SPAB, 1981.

RAMM, H.G., McDOWALL, R.W. and MERCER, ERIC. *Shielings and Bastles. HMSO, 1970.*

RAMSEY, S. and HERVEY, J. *Small Georgian Houses and their Details.* Architectural Press, 1972.

REED, MICHAEL. *The Georgian Triumph, 1700-1830.* Paladin, 1983.

REID, RICHARD. *The Shell Book of Cottages.* Michael Joseph, 1977.

ROBERTSON, CHARLES. *Bath: An Architectural Guide.* Faber and Faber, 1975.

SINCLAIR, COLIN *Thatched Houses of the Old Highlands.* Oliver and Boyd, 1953.

SMITH, P. *Houses of the Welsh Countryside.* HMSO, 1975.

STERNE, L. *Tristram Shandy.* 1767.

STEVENS, JOAN. *Old Jersey Houses.* Five Oaks Press, 1965.

SUMMERSON, JOHN *Georgian London.* Barrie and Jenkins, 1962.

SWIFT, J. *Directions to Servants,* 1731. Published 1745.

TATE, W.E. *The English Village Community.* Victor Gollancz, 1967.

THOMPSON, E.P. *The Making of the English Working Class.* Penguin, 1975.

TOMLIN, M. *English Furniture.* Faber and Faber, 1972.

TRENT, CHRISTOPHER. *England in Brick and Stone.* Anthony Blond, 1958.

TREVELYAN, G.M. *English Social History.* Penguin, 1974.

ULSTER FOLKLIFE. Published by the Ulster Folk and Transport Museum. Volume 2, 1956.

182

DANACHAIR, C.O. *Three House Types*. McCourt, D. *The Outshut House-type and its Distribution in County Londonderry*. Volume 8 1962; GAILEY, A. *Two Cruck Houses near Lurgan;* McCOURT, D. *Weaver's Houses around South-west Lough Neagh*. Vols 15 and 16, 1970; McCOURT, D. *The House with Bedroom over/Byre: a long-house derivative*. Volume 22, 1976; GAILEY, A. *The Housing of the Rural Poor in Nineteenth-Century Ulster*.

WATKIN, DAVID. *Thomas Hope and the Neo-Classical idea*. John Murray, 1968; *The Buildings of Britain:* Regency. Barrie and Jenkins, 1982.

WEST, TRUDY. *The Timber-frame House in England*. David and Charles, 1971.

WILLIAM, EURWYN. *The Historical Farm Buildings of Wales*. John Donald Publishers Ltd, 1986.

WILLIAMS ELLIS, C. *Buildings in Cob, Pise and Stabilized Earth*. 1947.

WITTKOWER, RUDOLF. *Palladio and Palladianism*. George Braziller, 1974.

WOOD, J. Senior. *Essay Towards a Description of Bath*. 1749.

WOOD, J. Junior. *Series of Plans for Cottages or Habitations of the Labourer*. 1781.

WOODFORDE, JAMES. Late eighteenth-century diary, edited by John Bereford as *The Diary of a Country Parson*. Oxford, 1931.

WOODFORDE, JOHN. *The Truth about Cottages*. New edition, Routledge and Kegan Paul, 1979; *Georgian Houses for All*. Routledge and Kegan Paul, 1985.

WRIGHT, L. *Clean and Decent*. Routledge and Kegan Paul, 1960.

YARWOOD, DOREEN. *The English House*. B.T. Batsford Ltd, 1979; *English Interiors: A Pictorial Guide and Glossary*. Lutterworth Press, 1983.

Index

190